The Textile Design Book

$\frac{1}{10}$

URAL OWL.
SYRNIUM URALENSE.

English-language edition first published
in 1988 in the United States of America by
Lark Books,
50 College Street,
Asheville, North Carolina, 28801
ISBN 0-937274-83-6

and in Great Britain by
A & C Black (Publishers) Ltd.
35 Bedford Row
London WC1R 4JH
ISBN 0-7136-5054-0

English translation © 1988 Lark Books

© 1986 Karin Jerstorp and Eva Kohlmark

First published in Sweden under the title
Forma Monster by Bonnierfakta
Bokforlag AB, Stockholm

Translated from the Swedish by
Inger Harrison for Net Works, Inc.

Production: Down Cusick
Typesetting: Diana Deakin

Library of Congress Catalog Card
Number: 87-46242

Reprinted 1990, 1992, 1995

Paperback edition 2000

Printed in Slovenia by DELO tiskarna
by arrangement with Korotan Ljubljana

Photos:
Nisse Backman, studio eighty three, page 8,
9, 10, 11, 13, 20, 21, 25, 36, 39, 41, 45, 47,
49, 56, 58, 65, 67, 73, 74, 75, 80, 82, 89,
91, 100, 107, 110, 112, 114, 115.
Marionettmuseet, Stockholm, page 9
 (shadow puppet)
Roger Stenberg/Mira, page 15 (forest)
Joe Lindstrom, page 29, 98 (water tower)
Klas-Rune Johansson/Naturfotograferna
 page 42 (firewood pile)
Nisse Peterson, front cover.

KARIN JERSTORP   EVA KOHLMARK

The Textile
Design Book

Understanding and creating

patterns using texture, shape,

and color.

A & C BLACK
LONDON

Contents

Course participants who contributed ideas and sketches:

Toshiko Aoi	Barbro Hjort af Ornas	Gerda Ljungstedt	Monica Westberg	Class 7, Hasselby Villastads school
Ann Engstrand	Hedel Holmboe	Bodil Sterner	Ingrid Wikars	Course in designing, Komvux, Stockholm
Vivi Eriksson	Benita Jansson	Birgitta Soderberg	Birgit Zelmerloow	Course in weaving, Komvux, Ekero
Kerstin Hauglid	Magdalena Karlsson	Lisa Wahlstrom	Birgitta Oberg	

There was a time
when each one made a work of art
at the same time as a useful thing
and out of this uniting
burst a spontaneous joy.

William Morris

It is this joy over the collaboration between one's hands, imagination, and eyes that we are going to revive with **The Textile Design Book**. We realize the need for a book with a lot of ideas which provides inspiration and shows how you can sketch and form patterns for all kinds of projects.

The Textile Design Book teaches you to discover and be inspired by the smallest fragments of nature or your own luncheon sandwich. The exciting exercises with unconventional materials and completely new ways of making sketches and models will help you achieve surprisingly quick results. They will make designing more pleasurable, even for the inexperienced, and will encourage more use of patterns and decorations. All exercises with stripes, squares, borders, textures and stylized decorations include sketches using different handicraft techniques. We also show how one pattern can be varied and used in different ways.

In the chapter on color there are many playful exercises which will expand your knowledge about the variety of colors, their influence on each other, and their significance in patterns. You will find it fascinating to try different color combinations for your own patterns.

We hope the historical and international perspectives — both in words and pictures — will stimulate your interest in the past and in pattern making of other cultures.

We thank students and course participants who enthusiastically did our exercises and who provided sketches for illustrations in this book.

Karin Jerstorp   Eva Kohlmark

Sketching
with objects from nature

When you stroll through the forest and across fields you will discover that nature, with its rich variations and exquisite detail, is unsurpassed in color and patterns. Just envision the countryside during spring, with swelling buds, blossoming trees, and the changing colors of a hillside covered with wildflowers. Envision the summer meadow filled with flowers and blowing grasses, or the bright colors of autumn against a clear blue sky. Enjoy the soft colors of lichens and moss. Discover the beauty of the spent fields. See how vividly dry weeds and seedpods stand out against the snow. We hope you will view nature with fresh eyes, discovering the interaction of its infinite lines and forms.

Wander along to a field or a wooded hill. Pick flowers, leaves, branches, moss, weeds and mushrooms. Enjoy colors and forms, and touch all the surfaces: soft, rough, smooth, rugged. Have you ever used materials from nature in a weaving? If not, we think you should try it. It feels both free and fun to use flowers and weeds as weaving materials since one does not have to meet any demands for precision or quality. Almost without realizing it, you will train yourself to observe the different shades of green in plants. You will also discover the benefits of alternating between hard and soft materials in weaving.

Certain flowers and plants keep their color even if dried, but remember that fresh materials will shrivel as they dry, making the weaving looser. Look carefully when deciding what flowers and plants to pick.

Consider that it takes many years for moss to grow. In her book *Bildhuggarens dotter*, Tove Jansson writes: "If you step on moss once you will make a deep hole which does not spring up for a week. If you step once more you will have made a hole forever. The third time you step on the moss you will have killed it."

With nature as weft

You may make a warp to weave with by winding threads between two sticks. It is easier to work with if you hang up the sticks and stretch the warp by hanging weights from the lower stick. Weave by inserting grass, weeds, leaves and flowers over and under every other thread. The different materials may be woven either straight or at an angle, densely or sparsely. Weeds may protrude, fruits and berries may hang down. Let your imagination flow and work freely. Just make sure that the materials stay in the weaving. Good luck!

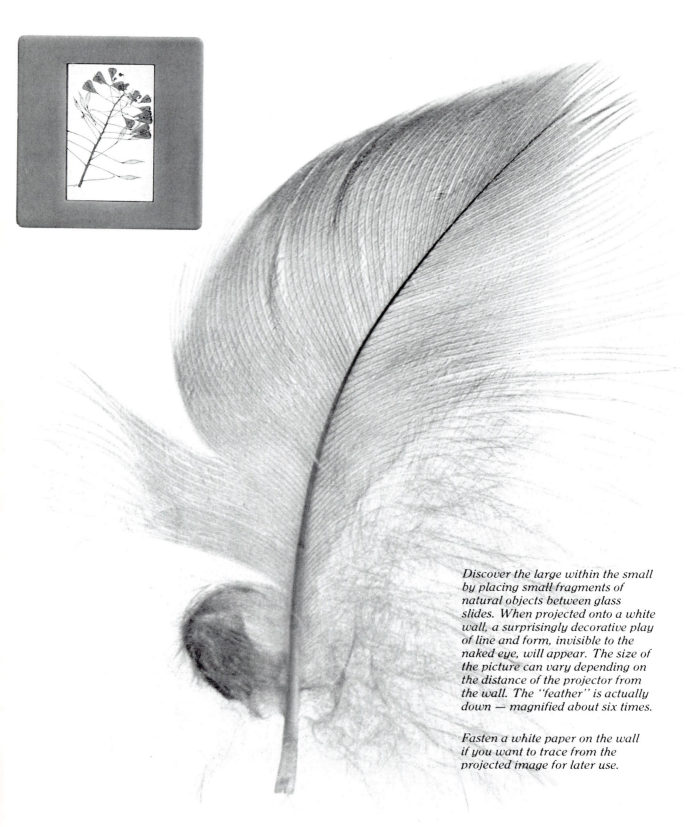

Discover the large within the small by placing small fragments of natural objects between glass slides. When projected onto a white wall, a surprisingly decorative play of line and form, invisible to the naked eye, will appear. The size of the picture can vary depending on the distance of the projector from the wall. The "feather" is actually down — magnified about six times.

Fasten a white paper on the wall if you want to trace from the projected image for later use.

Shadows and silhouettes

Man has always been fascinated by shadows and silhouettes. During prehistoric and medieval times, shadows played an important role; for example, the passing of time was measured using shadows. Shadowplay theater using dolls to make silhouettes against a see-through shade originated in the Orient. The shadowplay technique then spread across the rest of the world, reaching perhaps its highest development in Java, Indonesia and Burma.

During the 18th century it was popular to cut out silhouettes of black paper, placing them against a white background. This art form was popular until the middle of the 19th century when it was replaced by photography. Cutting silhouettes of trees, flowers, and birds is a well-known and appreciated folk art in Poland, where they also decorate the silhouettes with paper in different colors (see page 74). The art of cutting silhouettes was also practiced in Scandinavia.

The red cutout was executed in 1961 by Natalia Petterson from Himmelsberga on Oland in Sweden.

Impressions

At the seashore, footprints are washed away quickly by the waves — impressions of this kind are perishable, but fascinating when we find them

Shadow pictures as public decoration

The artist P.O. Ultvedt has decorated the subway station at Central Station in Stockholm by painting the projected silhouettes of some workers on the rugged rock wall.

It is gratifying to make impressions with different kinds of objects in a clay slab. This engraved, negative relief can, of course, be a decorative object in itself; however, it can also be used as a mold for a plaster of Paris casting, which then becomes an embossed (or raised), positive relief. The plaster of Paris relief shown left is done on a clay slab with an impression made by a pine branch.

The oldest decorations on clay pots were made by carving and impressions.

Collage of natural objects

Who has not occasionally collected beautiful seashells, rocks smoothed by the waves, aged wood pieces, or fragile seedpods? With fragments from nature you can play with many compositions. Organize the individual parts so they form a pleasing and exciting collage.

The collage can be hung on the wall as a summer memory or perhaps used as an inspiration for execution in a different technique.

By the 16th century the Italian artist Giuseppe Arcimboldo was painting portraits composed of collages of fish, fruit, flowers and vegetables.

Stripes

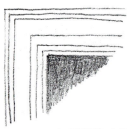

Have you ever thought about how many stripes there are in nature — in plants, insects, fish, mammals, rocks? You even have striped parts on your body, namely fingerprints which are so unique that they do not match those of anyone else.

Have you ever thought about how many striped things there are around us that are usually not thought of as patterns? We plow furrows and rake walkways to stir up the earth and gravel, and we make ice scrapers striped to create friction.

Have you thought

☐ that for practical reasons many building elements are made in narrow sections, giving a striped appearance to the finished product;

☐ that siding and clapboards give a house of wood a striped look;

☐ that heating elements give a striped impression because the material has been corrugated to give more surface;

☐ that the lumber used for making forms when pouring concrete gives the surface a somewhat striped effect. By laying the boards in different directions the surface design of concrete becomes varied;

☐ that moldings around doors and windows, and baseboards have a rich striped pattern for aesthetic, but also sometimes for practical, reasons.

☐ that picture frames and book spines often have a striped appearance.

Look around you and collect your own examples of stripes.

Flower colors furnished the inspiration for a striped sweater knitted in heavy yarn.

Definitions of stripes

When a surface is divided into larger and smaller sections by vertical and horizontal or diagonal lines, it produces a striped effect.

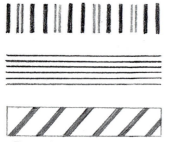

Densely placed smaller figures can also appear as stripes. Note that the stripe containing the largest number of small parts is the most obvious striped pattern.

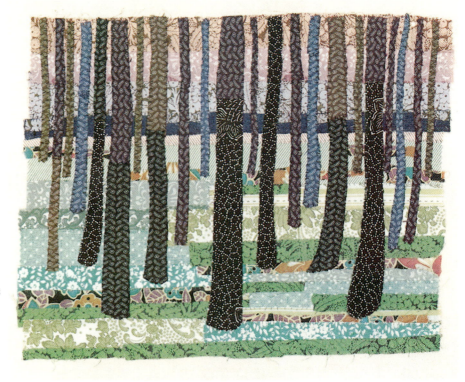

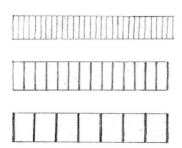

Lines can be repeated on surfaces, evenly spaced from each other, so that everything from densely to sparsely striped patterns appear.

Varying the line widths and the spaces between the lines creates many different patterns.

Varied lines can also be collected in groups which then are repeated regularly.

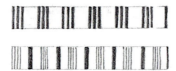

Each group may be symmetrical or asymmetrical.

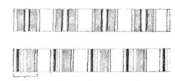

The mirror image of an asymmetric striping together with the original striping makes a symmetric pattern.

In a symmetrical group, the lines are spaced uniformly around an axis (the lines are mirror image). Avoid mixing symmetrical and asymmetrical groups of lines in the same pattern since they have such different characteristics. The symmetrical group seems static, while the asymmetrical moves your eyes from one group to the next group.

**Stripes inspired by nature
and pictures**

*This magazine picture of tree
trunks in a dusky forest has been
transformed to an application in
textiles, inventively constructed of
horizontal and vertical fabric
strips. The pattern of the strips
contributes effectively to the feeling
of the rough bark and scented*
◁ *woodland.*

▷ *Let yourself be inspired by an
environment, an animal, or an
object. Squint, look at the colors,
collect yarns you can use as
sampling materials. For textile
stripes, it is effective to wrap yarn
around a piece of cardboard. Try
to match the colors of the object
when choosing colors. The thin
legs of the redlegs suggested
working with sewing thread. The
speckled-feathered costume is
reproduced by twisting black and
white sewing thread together
before winding.*

*The elegant fan with its clear
colors in strong contrast to black,
represents the fairytale image
of Japan.*

Generally, we think of stripes as color changes. Stripes can also appear by changing techniques or by alternating texture or structure. Achieving stripes by changing techniques is often used in weaving and knitting by placing plain sections next to textured sections, dense sections against more open ones, and patterned sections against unpatterned.

Stripes formed by changing textures are often found in textiles, but also in many hard materials, for example, in wood and metal. On the Lapps' knife handles, the striped decorations are formed by inlaying alternate thin layers of horn, wood, birchbark, pewter, or leather.

You can make stripes by alternating shiny and dull or rough and smooth materials.

Stripes can also appear by alternating decorated sections with plain ones. Examined closely, this kind of striping might appear as a border effect, but seen from a distance the border pattern seems to disappear and reappear as stripes in divergent colors or textures.

Certain weaving techniques automatically produce a striped surface. Older rugs were woven in warp-faced ribs, where the thin warp completely covered the thick weft. By alternating the weft with a thick and a thin yarn, the surface achieves a pronounced horizontal striping.

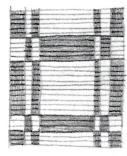

On the other hand, dukagang (a laid-in Swedish technique) gives a vertical striping to different pattern sections of the weavings, while twill and inlay weave give diagonal stripings.

Dukagang   *Twill*

Stripes can also encircle, decorating a pot, a bowl, or the perimeter of a plate.

Horizontal stripes around the human body are not always attractive. The pattern may look like rings, making the body resemble a barrel with its bands. On the other hand, vertical stripes may be flattering, gathered at the waist, then flowing out in soft pleats as you move.

A patterned effect can also be obtained by changing striped surfaces in different ways.

To achieve attractive stripes, it is important to balance the spacing between lines and groups of lines carefully. Avoid automatically making stripes and the spaces between them the same width; avoid making one stripe exactly half the width of the other one.

A striped pattern can appear completely different depending on whether it is viewed close up or from a distance. The tendency of the eye to want to "read together" at a distance forms and colors that are in some way related to each other can give the artist many surprises.

A dense pattern with a lot of contrast in lightness can blur at a distance. If you move the striped surface even farther away, it can appear to be all one color (also see page 136).

Painted stripes

For this exercise you will need water colors, flat brushes in different widths, and a slightly absorbent paper. Play with your favorite colors, making wide and narrow tracks with the brush. Paint densely and sparsely, symmetrically or asymmetrically.

When you concentrate on towels, as in this case, for a "first weaving," you can emphasize the shorter ends with narrow strips, so the towel won't look like just a small piece of a larger whole. The diagonally striped towels can be designed for printed fabric or terry cloth.

Methodical stripe exercises

Much can be learned about the nature of stripes by working with paper strips in three shades of the same color against a white background. The variations are endless — a slight movement of the strips can completely change the character of the pattern.

1. In this exercise, all color strips are cut to the same width. The white sections may be any width you choose.
   The striped sections "a" and "b" appear to curve, especially from a distance. The passing from light to dark produces a shadow effect. This effect disappears in group "c" by adding the narrow, white stripes.
2. By moving the darkest strips, an entirely new pattern appears.
3. Every shade has its own width. This invites you to build up irregular groups of stripes. If this is repeated regularly, the stripes take on a clear and distinct pattern effect.
4. If you substitute another color for the white background, for example, gold, the eye suddenly reads together blue-yellow groups of stripes, which appear to stand out from the light blue background.
5. By moving the gold surfaces, making the light blue stripes smaller and dividing the larger blue surfaces with narrow, clear orange stripes, the pattern again appears to be flat.
6. Completely irregular stripes cut in a bright color, in this case blue, against a white background. The pieces have been moved here and there, have exchanged places and have been shifted until the stripes, in spite of their irregularity, look evenly distributed across the surface.

Stripes like these can be colored, can be viewed lengthwise or crosswise, can be stretched out flat or be wavy. These may be used as a base for a composition for many different techniques — for example: carved into clay, etched into glass, executed in weaving and knitting. Use them to form loose, tight, or patterned sections.

Create completely different stripe designs with the same amount of color.

The colors from the red onion can be used in exercises in three different shades of red — burnt umber, mauve, and light clear rose. In examples 1, 2 and 3, each color has the same amount of combined area.

1. The stripes are built symmetrically around a burnt umber center strip. The pattern is only reproduced once, it only returns once. If you put a mirror along the outermost rose strip you can see the stripes repeated.
2. Each stripe section is irregularly constructed but is repeated regularly with even spacing between. How big is the repeat? Look carefully.
3. With equal amounts of each color you can also produce a completely irregular stripe pattern.
4. A color which diverges in shade and strength has been introduced at the expense of the light rose color. You can see right away that the new, vibrant, almost loud color gives the stripe pattern a completely different character. If you work with cut strips, it is easy to change and to try colors with each other without running the risk of "destroying" the original design with new colors.

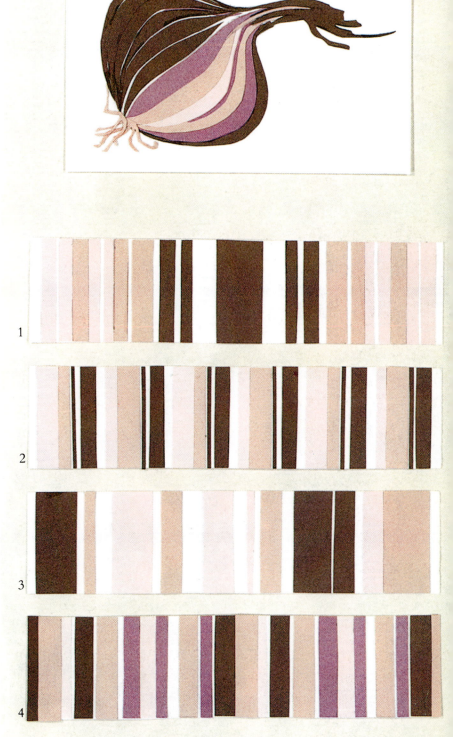

Stripes inspired by objects

This exercise is going to show how everyday objects in our surroundings may allow us to release our creativity. Before we hungrily devour the sandwiches, they will lend us their color combinations for some exercises. First, try to collect yarns in the "right" colors. The fun starts when you wrap and try them, hold them at a distance and contemplate. Squint your eyes to get an idea of how the stripes will appear. Sometimes let the lighter colors or the darker colors dominate — in narrow stripes or wide stripes, in regular or irregular patterns.

The exercise can be extended by "weaving" plaids with a large needle on a cardboard piece — in one case with the colors of the egg, in the other with the color of the anchovies. The woven piece can then be brushed a little to give you the illusion of an already finished fabric.

Cutouts

Try to capture some of the hues of autumn in a quick watercolor sketch. Then paint irregular stripes with the sketch's different details as a starting point. The aster might be a source for purple stripes, the rock for a rose.

Some of them may suit an old sofa which is crying out for a new cover. Draw the sofa on a sheet of paper and then cut out the upholstered sections of the sofa. You now have a model to superimpose on the top of the different stripe patterns.

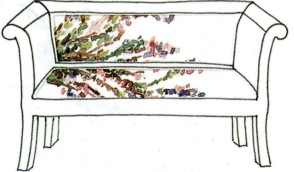

It is refreshing to see the unexpected stripes on a sofa style which is traditionally covered in fabric with rigidly recurring repeats. An irregular stripe gives a uniform feeling if it is well-balanced. Also, put the cutout on top of the water color to see how the sofa will look dressed in a large-flowered print chintz. When it is not necessary that old furniture be dressed in authentic period fabrics, one may freely choose patterns and colors that are best suited for the setting.

Stripes from memories

Imagine weaving a rug where each stripe has a history. Use Grandmother Lisa's flowery aprons for narrow stripes, and the children's soft-washed and sun-bleached clothing for a harmonizing base color.

If this is the first rug you are weaving, you need a sketch or a work plan to follow. If you are sketching in a scale of 1:10, it means that each centimeter or inch on the paper represents 10 centimeters or inches on the rug. Begin by weighing the rags and figure out how far each color will go. Use colored papers in the same colors as the rags. Using the paper strips, work the color design to scale. Printed rags are easily reproduced on paper by using fat crayons and then painting with water-color on top. Cut the painted pieces of paper into narrow strips with which you can then experiment to get the pattern for the rug.

It is practical to work with strips since it is easy to combine them in different ways and thus get widely different patterns with a completely different character (see page 19).

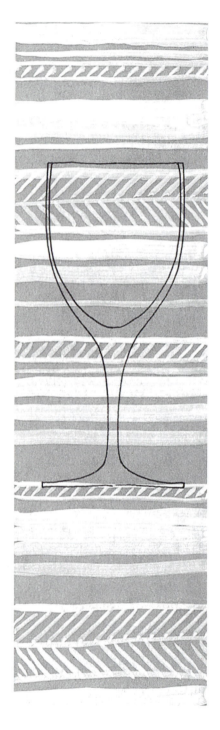

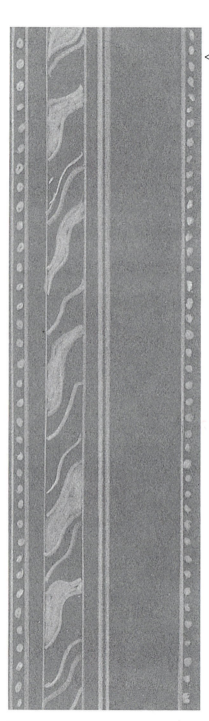

White on white

If you are going to decorate transparent materials such as glass, plastic, and thin textiles, you can sketch with opaque colors on parchment paper or with a white ink pen on gray paper. Then, if you want to see how the design harmonizes with the form of the object and where it will be suitable to place the design, you can draw the contour lines of the actual object on some clear plastic and superimpose it on the sketch.

Structure sketches

A striped decoration is often obtained by working in relief. It is one of the oldest ways of decorating clay objects and is also used for wood-cutting and in most textile techniques.

If you want to make sketches for these techniques, it works well to use papers with different structure such as corrugated paper, craft paper, and textured wallpaper. Corrugated paper comes in many different weights, and the stripes of the paper can be exploited in different ways. Don't forget that many papers have an interesting and useful reverse side.

Clay pot from Italy with zig-zag borders in relief, about the 7th century B.C.

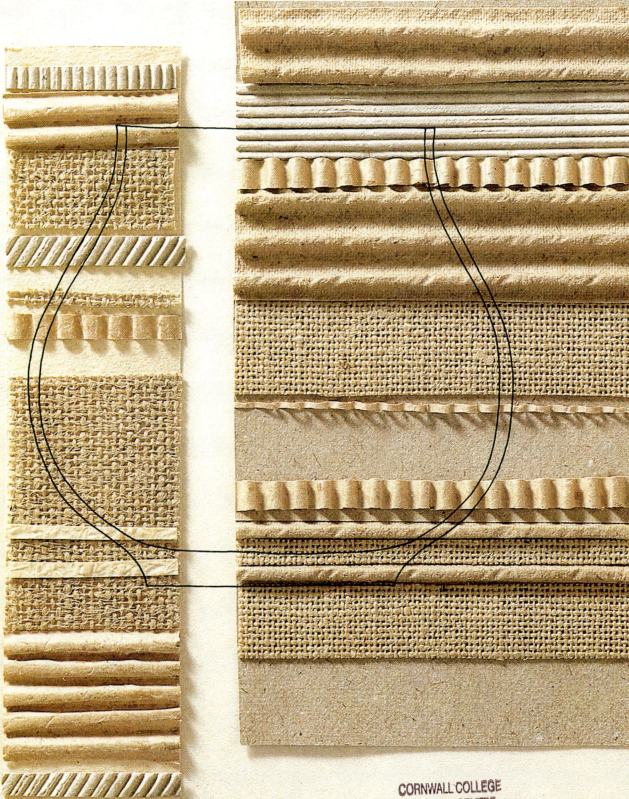

Period furniture

The color scale of furniture fabrics during different periods has changed and the preferred colors themselves have changed in strength and lightness. If you want to be faithful to the original style of the furniture, you have to keep this is mind when choosing furniture fabric.

The Gustavian period (about 1775 -1810) had a predilection for light and airy colors in stripes and checked furniture fabrics made out of linen and cotton. The fabric for the Gustavian chair is woven in handspun and hand dyed linen from about 100 years ago. Even today, you would probably have to both spin and dye yarns yourself to get the same vivid character.

The colors on the upper right were common during the end of the 18th century. The oil paint was thin and was brushed on lightly so that the grain of the wood showed faintly through the paint.

In the Karl Johan period (about 1810 -1840), dark furniture was covered with smooth linen and wool blends. The wide symmetrical striped sections divided the often very long sofas in an advantageous way. The color range was somewhat subdued, but the character of the pattern was clear and distinct. The illustrated striped fabric for the Karl Johan chair is made of strips cut from colored magazine pictures.

Stripes for decoration

When creating patterns, you also have to consider the function of the project. If you gradually change the proportions or the

colors in the stripes, the surface will appear to be curved. A rug has to lie flat and therefore cannot give the impression of differences in level. On the other hand, a striped design that curves can be pleasing for a curtain where the same change in proportions and colors gives the effect of generous, abundant, billowing fabric.

As can be seen from the pictures, even the width seems

to change — dark sections seem more narrow than the light ones.

Straight lines are almost always more pleasing for billowing fabric, while winding stripes can look like crawling snakes.

When the fabric is pleated or gathered, the effect completely changes, especially with vertical stripes when certain colors or stripes disappear in the pleat giving a less desirable effect. In the fashion field, this effect is often exploited on purpose.

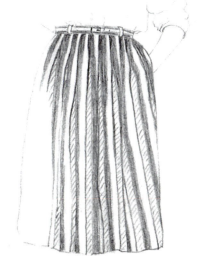

What is stark and plain on a flat surface can become soft and attractive on a curved surface. Notice how the stripes slink around the cone-shaped corner of the tablecloth. The tightly striped towel gives an inviting feeling if we put the hanger on the longer side.

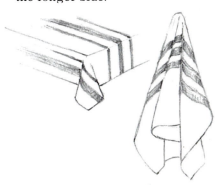

The scale of the stripes has to be adapted to the object and its function. Wide stripes are harder to match on a small object. Sometimes it might feel liberating when the pattern is out of scale; irregular and unexpectedly placed stripes can be refreshing, daring, and stylish.

Stripes can be distinct or vague, of even width and strong, or uneven and fragile, coarse, or hairsbreadth fine. They can be rigid and straight, or billow and twine softly and fade away. Sometimes it is hard to draw the line between stripes and free-form patterns across the surface.

By putting small figures in front of the sketch, you will suddenly see a completely new scale; at the same time it shows us an entirely new method of application. The simple stripe pattern has become a monumental ornamentation.

Stripes as pictures

Thanks to well-balanced colors and proportions, this simple composition of three horizontal solid-colored fields, has achieved both space and depth.

Paint papers in muted colors, then tear them into different width strips. Join them together to form a surface that makes exciting line plays appear. The soft torn strips "hide" the strips and we see a landscape which can be a tapestry or perhaps the decoration on a turned bowl.

Fun to know

The zebra is a striped animal. The eye-catching striped appearance of the zebra is in reality an excellent camouflage in the shadowplay under the acacias on the savannah.

Victor Vasarely, Zebras

Monumental stripes decorate the water towels in Kuwait, designed by Sune Lindstrom, Stockholm.

In many civilizations, narrow strips are woven with primitive tools. The strips are then joined together into a larger piece of fabric. In Africa, the strips are often decorated with cross-stripes and figures. When joined, the pattern produced a checked effect. A stripe has become a square.

Papermaking started in the beginning of the 19th century using rags. People were required to sell their rags to the industry for little compensation. When, in the later part of the 19th century, paper began to be made from wood and cellulose, the population was able to use its own textile rags for themselves. The weaving of rag rugs quickly became popular, especially Swedish striped rag rugs. Originally, the rugs were not meant to be stepped on, but were used only for decoration on festive occasions.

Squares

In nature there are no straight lines, and any squares that appear are soft and irregular. Observing this, we are inclined to say that it is man who discovered the square and the straight line. Man has always strived to order his life and art along straight lines and squares, beginning thousands of years ago, knotting nets and plaiting rugs and baskets in squares.

We are brought up from an early age to conform to various square systems. Who does not remember the square blue school notebooks, which had to be filled with numbers year after year, or home economics class when gingham was turned into gym bags, handiwork or school-kitchen aprons; or all the children's games: tic-tac-toe, checkers, battleship, mazes; or the games played during recess: hopscotch and ball games played on squares drawn on the ground.

Our dwellings are blocks, laid down or upright, decorated with windows in square shapes. Today window design varies from many paned squares of glass framed by white curtains and geraniums to the windows of the turn of the century with squares, diamonds, and geometric shapes of all kinds, with different colored glass in each square, to the wider expanse of glass used in picture windows.

We build square, half-timbered houses, lay brick walls in different patterns, make brick walkways and patios with different designs, and decorate floors and walls with fieldstone, wood, tile or concrete. In other civilizations, for example in China and Japan, the square has been varied in an inventive and elegant way as seen in these shoji screens made of rice paper.

If you are flying on a clear day, the landscape below looks like a quilt, and the streets of a city resemble a net of squares. Selma Lagerlof describes the thoughts of Nils Holgersson while he was flying over Skane like this: "Then he understood, that the large, checkered fabric was the flat countryside of Skane, which he was flying across. And he started to understand why it looked so multi-colored and checkered. The bright green squares he recognized first: they were the rye fields, which had been planted last fall and had stayed green under the snow. The yellow-gray squares were stubble fields, where last summer grain had grown; the brownish were old clover-fields, and the black were empty pastures or plowed fields."

Picture-inspired square pattern

Sometimes we may be especially drawn to a picture. It may be the mood, the motif, or the colors which attract us. Begin with such a picture; catch the colors and the proportions, maybe also a specific form, and transform the picture into a pattern.

A picture of a camel's head might make us experience the warmth, the sand, and the bellow of the camel in the oasis outside Aswan. The color of the camel, the narrow dark stripe by his eye, and his haughty look have inspired squares in soft colors, with narrow distinct stripes which intersect each other.

Checks and squares

A checked surface occurs when two lined systems intersect and form straight or slanting angles. Sometimes it is the lines that form the pattern; sometimes the square is the prime element and the lines have less significance.

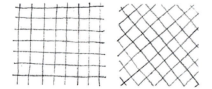

Lines form checked patterns

˘ The most common patterns in weaving are formed when groups of threads of different colors and width cross. The checked pattern can also be built on the difference in each section: the contrast between the denseness and the looseness, or the contrast in structure or materials, or in combinations of these.

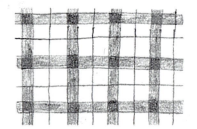

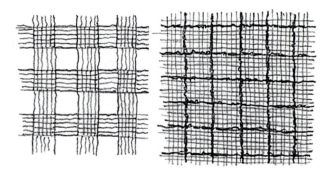

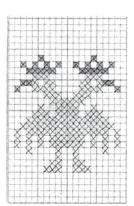

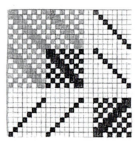

Checkered net as foundation

With a simple right angle checkered net as a foundation, you can create patterns for many textile techniques including counted cross stitch, knitting, crochet, beadwork, and embroidery over counted threads. The whole weaving theory with its many complicated tie-ups can be visualized in graphic patterns on graph paper.

The square as a pattern element

Many handicraft techniques are structured so that the square — solid-colored or in different colors — is repeated in a regular way in height and width so that the decorative surface is formed. In this way, we make patterns in stone and parquet floors, tiled walls, and even many ceilings.

Overlapped squares

Brick walls consist of rectangular bricks which have been overlapped in relationship to each other in many different ways. Each different way of laying brick has its specific name. The illustration shows the running bond and the English bond.

English bond

Running bond

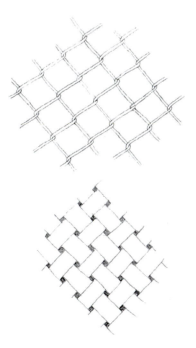

Squares on the Bias

If the lines cross each other on the diagonal, diamond shaped squares will appear. Glass is often cut in this pattern, and it is also the basis of argyle knitting. Even birch bark and chip-baskets are often made this way so that diagonal squares are formed.

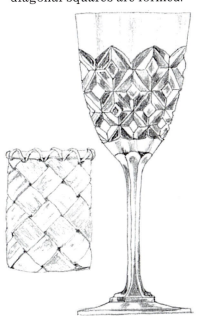

Squares can be so interesting.

Decorated squares

The decorated square with a geometric, stylized, or abstract motif forms a pattern in itself, but if it is joined with other similar squares it can also form new patterns (see pp. 49, 52, 53). Tiles for floors and walls are often laid in this way, and many quilts are based on this principle. In decorative art, it is common to adapt plant, animal, and human figures into geometric patterns, often square or rectangular (see p. 114 and 115). To create decorative squares like this demands both imagination and the ability to stylize, as well as sure line control.

Word-inspired squares

Just as a picture can inspire you to create, so a poetic word can inspire you to think in colors and forms.

In a group that is going to weave afghans, the participants might each get a slip of paper with an evocative, poetic word; for example, sea swells, south wind, red-breasted robin. "Sunbeam" might give someone an impression of a narrow light stripe which breaks through darker colors. "A forest glade" might evoke many different shades of green.

Without revealing the word you are working with, design an afghan on paper so that the colors and design correspond to your word. It is also important to show the soft character of the afghan. One sketch could be colored with crayons on coarse paper, another could be painted with water-colors. Together the group looks at the sketches, and you let the others guess what word was your inspiration.

(Evening)

(Seaside meadow)

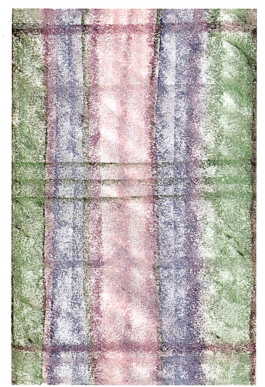

Painting through reflection

In this exercise, the object is to paint irregular squares for a weaving in such a way that you can see the colors blend where the stripes cross each other. Think about using colors that do not cover each other, but rather, blend. The plaid pattern, even if it is unbalanced, is important because the proportion of colors allows you to visualize how it will look when completed or as a fourth of a tablecloth, scarf, or afghan. By angling two mirrors at one of the corners, you can see where it is best to place the center of the design.

Painting to go with your china

This exercise is to paint plaids that match your china pattern — a graceful, elongated pattern for elegant china, a rustic, country look for the everyday cup.

Here, the same idea applies as when coloring a pattern for a towel; the fabric should give a feeling of completeness and should not look as if it is cut out of a larger piece (see p. 17). Drawing the pattern denser or thinner toward the edges can enhance a feeling of completeness.

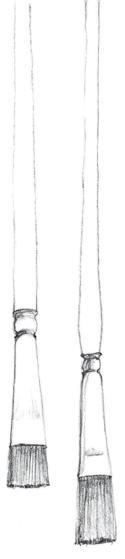

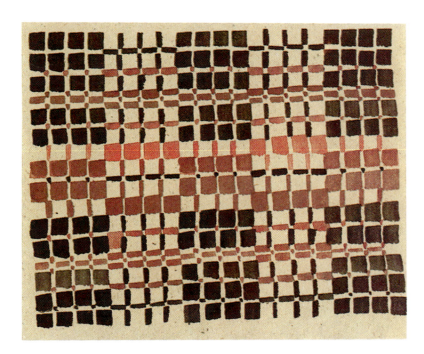

Color squares with a flat brush

Many weaving patterns are built on squares. With the help of flat brushes in different widths, you can easily paint narrow and wide squares. Each flat brush can leave both wide and narrow tracks depending on how the brush is held.

First, paint the background colors on the paper. They can be monochrome, striped, checked, or muted. Organize the brush-strokes in groups across the painted backgrounds using the technique for which you plan to use the sketch (For example: plaid, monk's belt, or double weave.)

The sketch on the left, opposite page, is meant for monk's belt on a background that is muted. The sketch above, in an old-fashioned color scheme painted on rag-paper, is meant to be executed as a wool plaid on an unbleached linen background.

Note how different the same type of weave appears in light pastel colors on the table-runner below.

Hold the folds towards the light occasionally and check for pleasing proportions.

Lightly fasten the folds at random with a gluestick before you fold the paper in the other direction.

Very thin lines can be drawn with felt-tip pens.

Folding with tissue paper

To achieve a checked effect quickly and easily, fold tissue paper lengthwise and then crosswise. Because the tissue paper is transparent, it seems darker at the folds where it is three layers thick and even darker when it is folded the other way, since it will be six layers thick at the intersections. This is a good way of designing striped and checkered patterns for light, transparent textiles.

Begin by folding relatively light tissue paper. Do not use anything smaller than a letter size sheet, since each folding decreases the size of the paper. Make sure the outer edges coincide to get the folds perpendicular across the paper. Do not draw where you want the folds, but instead fold across a standard letter size sheet.

Stark, white folds also stand out beautifully against a dark background. Papers in different colors can be put together before folding. Fasten the previous folds lightly at each corner against thin white paper, which you then hold up to a window pane so the transparency is clearly evident. ▷

The colors of the wintry wood pile in the picture inspired the interlacement in the picture at the left.

Woven plaids

Plaid objects are as common now as in past civilizations. By weaving plant fibers, leather, birch bark, hair, yarns, and narrow fabric strips, man has made baskets, rugs, sails, shoes, hats, bags, and jewelry. In museums all over the world, you can see how primitive people constructed the most complicated interlaced patterns.

By weaving with paper strips, we can make samples of many of today's handicraft techniques, for example: drall, double weave, work with leather and splints, and so on.

Paint large sections of paper with water colors and cut them into strips of different widths. Decide what order you want the warp to be in (in what order the vertical paper strips should be) and fasten them down lightly in the margin at the top of your paper with a little space between each strip. Then, begin by weaving in horizontal strips to form a checkered pattern. With the help of two white paper squares (see illustration, page 42) you can then clearly define the section of the pattern that is most pleasing to you. Also, try placing two mirrors at right angles to see if the pattern would benefit from being repeated symmetrically. Read more about mirror reflection on pages 63 and 67.

The symmetrical plaid to the left might work effectively for a totebag or, on a different scale, a privacy screen or windbreak made of rough-cut lattice strips.

A woven plaid is also the basis for the application below. The long, narrow squares and the pale colors take your thoughts to a cityscape. The urban mood is heightened by the small, black squares.

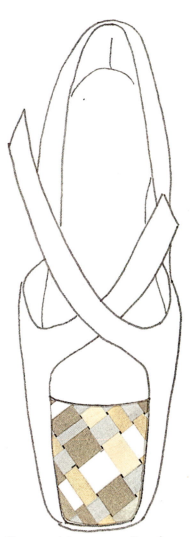

Here a quiet, square pattern has been transferred to the leather upper of a shoe.

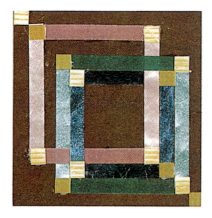

Interlacements gift wrap ribbons

Houndstooth pattern

Methodical weaving for fun

Weaving with giftwrapping ribbon demands a degree of dexterity since the ribbons are shiny and slippery, but the results are surprisingly elegant. The surface can be completely covered, but you can also introduce an extra dimension by laying a matching paper underneath it. The shine of the material makes us think of jewels and enamel work.

Conscious color changes in "warp and weft directions" produce well-known patterns in weaving. The so-called "houndstooth" pattern above is found all over the world in both woven and plaited works.

You can weave with variegated, one-colored, or patterned strips, with strips cut from magazine pictures or with strips for different textured papers. They can be cut or torn, straight, or gracefully and consciously shaped. They can be wrinkled or consist of twisted or braided paper towels. Experiment with different materials.

You can weave straight or askew, dense or sparse. The "weft" can jump across one, two, or more warp strips at one time or maybe protrude as loops on top of the surface. Play and have fun!

In about 1980, the American artist Marjorie Graham Trout created the humorous, soft sculpture in velvet velvet and plush, which she calls "Closely Woven Family." It is made up of 16 separately constructed parts which she then wove together so it seems as if the people are embracing each other endlessly.

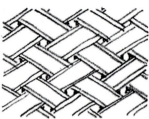

Diagonals

In some special weaving techniques, such as goose eye and korndrall, a diagonal check appears. The diagonal-square pattern is also a cherished pattern in knitting, where the argyle pattern is worked in many variations on socks and sweaters.

The style of the southern and central Lapp culture of Sweden is characterized by geometric decorations that completely cover the surface. Objects made of everything from spoons to the tips of skis are decorated with carved patterns, loosely interwoven lines having straight or diagonal angles. The spaces between the lines are decorated with two or four knife cuts.

The lively sketch for a rug has as its origin a paper which has been painted with diagonal stripes. This paper has been cut into squares and strips which then have been joined together in a new way so that squares appear. Try to create squares and stripes yourself in a similar way.

A surface from squares

Patterns for many needlecrafts, such as cross-stitch, petit point, and bargello are designed on graph paper.

Counted cross-stitch, with all its variations, is one of the oldest and most widely used needle arts. The embroidery is usually done on a light, solid background in borders, letters, and pattern groups. This kind of needlework has been found in Egyptian Coptic graves of the mid-11th century A.D. The Old English cross-stitch pattern below illustrates this type of pattern. Small black squares are skillfully built into a symmetrical pattern in a circular form.

decorated furniture and all kinds of objects in the middle-class home. Cross-stitch naturally lends itself to geometric patterns such as the houndstooth motif and the modern suspenders demonstrate.

Cross-stitch can also be worked so that it covers the whole background, so that each stitch is seen only as part of the whole. These examples of needle arts are preserved from the 13th century. With enough small squares, it is possible to create very realistic patterns. The suspender on the far right from the 1880s and the pouch (a sewing bag) represent a pattern which during this period

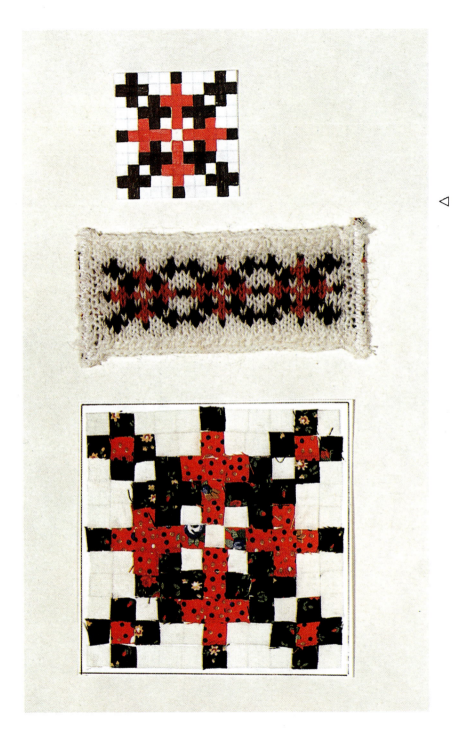

Designing on graph paper

Graph paper and colored or felt tip pens are all that are needed for this exercise. Begin with an uneven number of squares, for example 11 x 11 or 13 x 13. Use only a few colors. Start at the center square and create a pattern by repeating plus signs.

These square patterns can be repeated for borders or larger areas and can be converted into designs for embroidery, knitting, or quilting. They can also be used with hard materials (mosaic and beadwork) and in a larger format for a patterned tile floor.

When two or four of the same kind of patterned squares are joined together, new patterns are formed where the corners meet. You may consciously design the corners so that when joined, they give an interesting pattern. To give the surface more life and to avoid a rigid repeat you may connect many different squares.

Here, two different squares have been used in a border on knitted garments. On the purse cover, these squares are joined together to form a pattern to cover the entire surface, which has been worked in counted cross-stitch with many variations of moss green and dark rose.

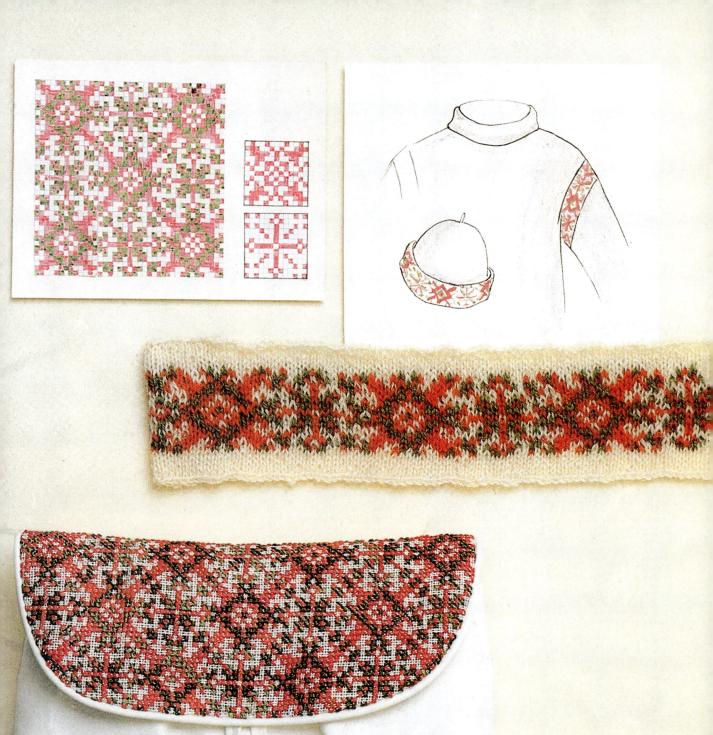

Paper cut-outs for a square

A simple cut-out exercise where you begin with a square will show how small cuts into the paper completely change the character of the pattern.

Lay four squres of black tissue paper, about 14 x 14 centimeters or 5½″ x 5½″, on top of each other. Fold them in half both ways, so the surface is divided into four smaller squares. Cut into the folded sides but leave the outer edges of the squares uncut. Unfold the papers and lift off the top sheet of paper.

Attach the cut-out on top of a white background. You will now have a *light* pattern which stands out against a black background.

Fold the remaining three sheets of paper again and this time cut into the straight outer edges. Unfold the papers and take off the top sheet. Attach this sheet to a white paper. You now have a *black* pattern which stands out against a white background.

The two remaining sheets of paper can be cut in half down the center or on the diagonal, so you now get four pieces out of each sheet of paper. These pieces can then be joined in a new way with a little space between for a variation of the larger square.

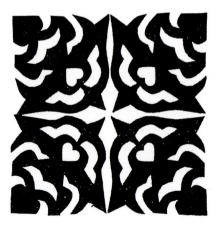

The pieces can also be used as a surface design.

The pattern can be enlarged or reduced. The scale of the pattern, the density, and the color scheme decide its usefulness for different techniques, for example: for damask weave or printing on paper or fabric.

On the picture to the right, the surface pattern is painted on transparent paper which then has been placed on top of blue cardboard.

Changes in patterns

When many similar squares are joined, new and often unexpected patterns are formed depending on your eyes' ability to "read together" surfaces with the same value, hue, intensity, or tint.

The quilt in the large picture is built up of squares. In each square an octagon (8 sides) is made which in its turn is divided into four light and four dark triangles. The light and dark triangles change places from square to square, but the small corner triangles are always light.

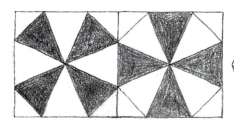

When the squares are joined together, the geometrically divided squares will magically disappear and your eye will instead see large, soft star formations, light circles or crosses.

When the impression changes in this way between different formations, we call the pattern unstable.

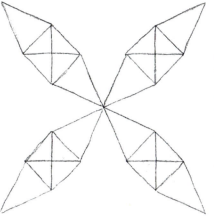

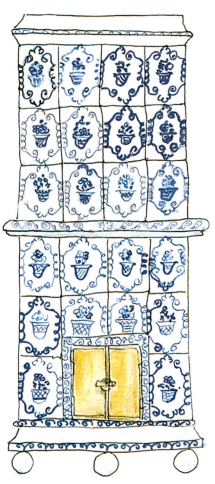

This 1914 tiled fireplace is made of handpainted, blue and white ceramic tiles. Each tile is decorated with a flower-filled bowl surrounded by arabesques. When you look at the pattern closely, you will discover that it is not only the blue color that changes in a lively way, but the bowls also have different patterns, and the flowers are not repeated exactly. Just this simple variation in color and detail, characteristic of handpainting, gives this repeated pattern life and charm.

Designing plant and animal motifs in a square

Formerly, it was common to design stylized plant, animal, and human figures in geometric forms. Here are some examples from different time periods using a variety of materials.

The picture below shows a stele, a rectangular grave or remembrance stone from Babylonia. This limestone from 2500 B.C. shows Sumerian warriors in leather hoods and long woolen skirts carrying spears and battle-axes. The picture is highly stylized and

skillfully designed inside the rectangular form.

Detail from a coffin from the end of the 12th century with decorations done in iron

forging from Rydaholm church in Smaland in Sweden. The coffin is now in Stockholm at the National History Museum.

This detail is from an early 15th century blue and white double weave, which is called a Grodinge-hanging. The mythical animals imprinted in the checked squares are probably adaptions from Persian-Byzantine silk fabrics. The wallhanging,

originally from the medieval church of Grodinge, is now in Stockholm at the National History Museum.

Detail from an embroidered travel pillow given to Karna Trulsdotter from Ostra Grevie as a wedding present in 1827 in Skane. The pillow is done in satin stitch embroidery with plant-dyed wool yarn on black fabric.

The floral motif which is enclosed in a rectangle is from the *Handbook of Plant and Floral Ornament* by Richard G. Hatton, which was first published in 1909. The pictures are from botanical works of the 16th century and show the most beautiful drawings of plants from this period. Each plant fills the rectangular area in both a naturalistic and

stylized way. These drawings were often used as patterns for woodcarvings and engravings in metal during that period.

Studies at museums

We can gain much inspiration from the pattern treasures which are kept in museums — great or small — all over the world.

Lilli Zickerman (1858 - 1949), who laid the foundation for the Swedish handicraft movement, carried out a gigantic inventory of Swedish textiles and peasant handicraft. Thirteen thousand objects were inventoried and documented in 24,000 photos, partially colored with the original colors. The studies of the shag rugs and pillows were made

Modern chain stitch embroidery on a wedding blanket from Iraq. Different sized squares and borders are completely covered by geometric patterns in bright, clear colors.

Museum study with water colors from a ceramic shard from the Near East, possibly 4,000 years old.
Study of a storage sack made from camel skin, which was common among the Tuaregs, a Berber tribe of the Western Sahara.

from Zickerman's colored photos by a textile student at the Knostfackskolan at the end of the 1940s. Copies were done in Indian ink and painted with water colors on transparent paper that was then "dry-pasted" to lay flat.

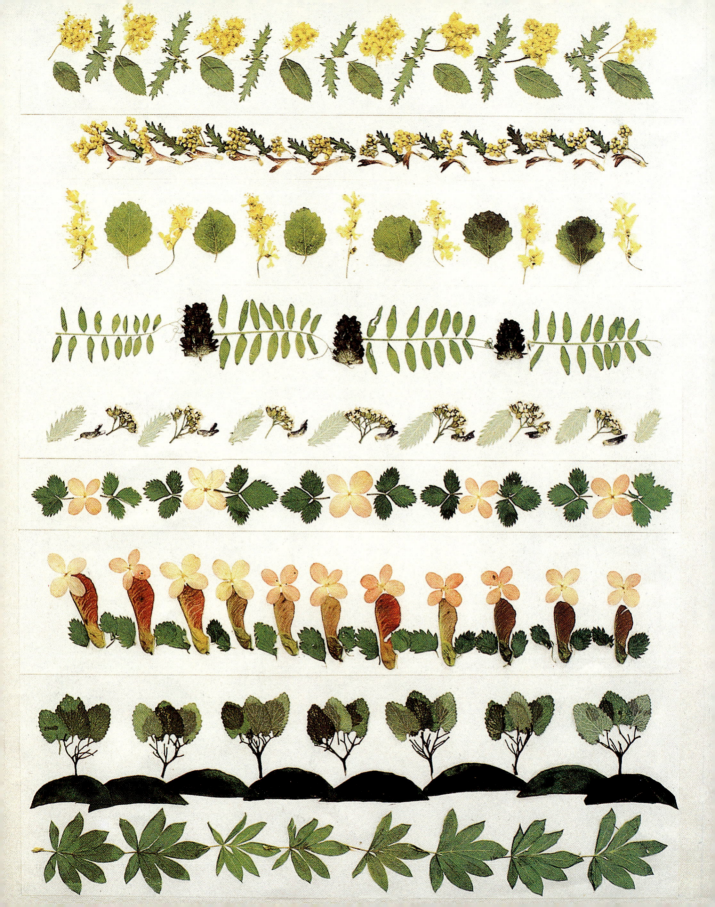

Borders

The border is probably the oldest way of decorating. It is formed by arranging ornaments next to each other in horizontal rows, or above and below each other in vertical lines. The word ornament comes from the Latin word "ornate" which means to adorn. In architecture the border is used as a frieze. In interior decorating and on furniture it appears as edging.

Nature has always been man's foremost inspiration for creating patterns. What he has taken from nature depended on which century, environment, and culture he lived in. Each generation has interpreted nature in its own way — transforming it into realistic, stylized, or geometric forms.

Originally each decoration had a symbolic meaning. For the ancient Egyptians, the lotus was the symbol of growth. When the river Nile receded after its yearly flooding, the lotus flower was the first to sprout from the fertile earth and, for that reason, it was seen as a promise of the coming ample harvests. The lotus flower, in blossom or in bud, stylized in the Egyptian manner, is found reproduced in the decorative arts in many different variations, century after century.

When creating a border you can start simply, by laying leaf next to leaf, flower next to flower, in rows. If you curve the row, you get a garland. It has been said that this is how boys in Indian weaving families learned the art of designing patterns. They picked apart fresh flowers and organized the leaves in rows and figures, which then took the forms of new flowers, becoming their own creations.

Do as the Indian boy does — pick flowers and leaves, combine them in different ways and organize them into rows and patterns against a white or colored background. Paste lightly and put in a press. Lay transparent paper on top of the borders and trace them.

A combination of two wild strawberry leaves and a river-beauty flower is repeated here for a border which decorates the stationery we might use for a note to a dear friend.
The border on the picture is handpainted, but it could very well be made with potato printing or stenciling if it needs to be repeated.

A little history

Creating patterns with simple geometric forms is the same around the world. From earliest times, certain forms have been used by all people to decorate body, clothing, and property. Even the simplest forms have had symbolic meaning. For example, the circle and the square have symbolized the sun or the universe and for that reason they have adorned ritual objects.

Sometimes similar patterns, such as the meandering arabesque, have turned up in different parts of the world, independent of each other.

Sometimes you can trace a pattern that has travelled from country to country, continent to continent. The Oriental arabesque, which can be everything from highly stylized flower vines to plaited decorations, was spread with the Crusaders from Egypt across Europe to Ireland, where it appeared mainly in books, then on to Scandinavia, where we find it in runic stones and woodcarvings. To this day, you can find this plaited decoration in twist embroidery and damask weave.

On Fair Isle, a small isolated island between the Shetland Islands and Orkney, traditional sweaters with brightly colored borders are knitted — sweaters that are well-known all over the world. Fair Isle patterns have Moorish and Spanish origins. One of the Spanish Armada ships was wrecked near Fair Isle in 1588. The ship was laden with objects such as knitted silk clothing with religious and national symbols. The islanders copied some of the motifs in their wool sweaters.

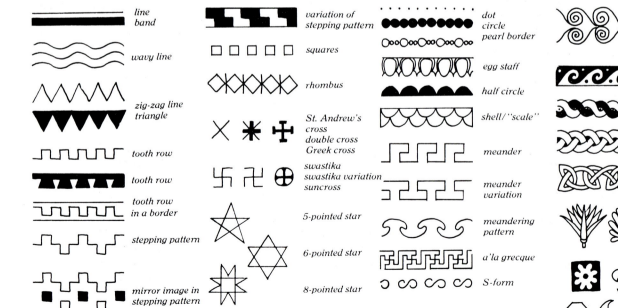

line band	variation of stepping pattern	dot circle pearl border	double spiral
wavy line	squares	egg staff	running dog
zig-zag line triangle	rhombus	half circle	cord
tooth row	St. Andrew's cross double cross Greek cross	shell/"scale"	braid
tooth row	swastika swastika variation suncross	meander	braided pattern
tooth row in a border	5-pointed star	meander variation	lotus bloss
stepping pattern	6-pointed star	meandering pattern	palm leaf
mirror image in stepping pattern	8-pointed star	a'la grecque	rosette
		S-form	fleur de lis
	St. George's cross Maltese cross	spiral	"elephant footprint" "summer squash" Ying-Yang

Borders are still knit with St. Andrew's crosses, Greek crosses, octagons, and the rose, the last also being a common motif in Oriental rugs.

 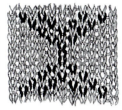

Greek cross   *St. Andrew's cross*

Most of these ornaments are thousands of years old. Yet they are still being used today and can be seen in the meandering arabesque on the "Marie" cookie, the arabesque rugbeaters, and the lotus blossom on the sewing machine. Truly, there is nothing new under the sun!

With renewed interest, study ornamentation and symbols on architecture, furniture, Oriental rugs, textiles of all kinds, picture frames, church murals, and so on. The happiness and satisfaction from a possible discovery will be well worth the trouble.

The rattan rugbeater used even today shows a neat arabesque whose form has its roots in Oriental art.

A 4,500-year-old Sumerian grave excavation shows that even in ancient Babylonia, forms from nature were used as a decorative art form. Here, rows of leaf-forms of hammered gold have been arranged for a necklace.

One of the illustrations in the original manuscript of the *Book of Kells* shows these skillfully drawn small figures plaited into each other. If you look more closely, you can discover that each figure represents the letter Q. Note the man whose toe tickles his neighbor's nose. Compare this drawn plaited work the from 8th century with the textile plaited sculpture from the 1980s on page 44.

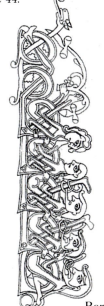

The fleece basket from Dalarna dates from the 13th century and is richly decorated with plaited ornaments. The basket is at the Scandinavian Museum in Stockholm.

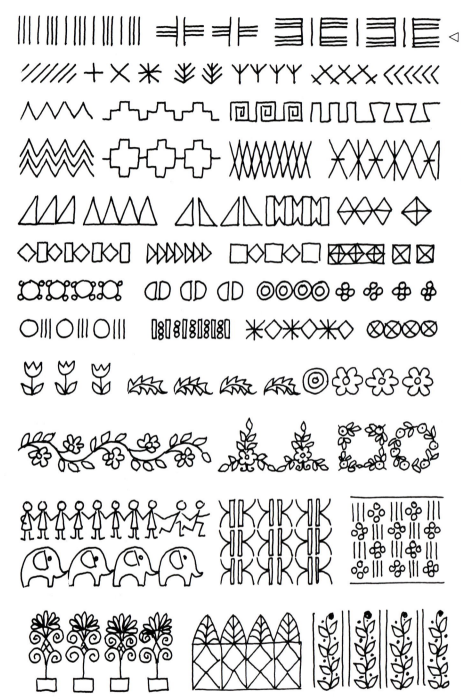

How to construct borders

Although many pattern ornaments are alike all over the world, there does not seem to be any limit to man's imagination when it comes to varying them. Traditionally, the ornaments fall into certain categories, including geometric ornaments, plant and animal ornaments, figure and object ornaments, and ornaments that combine two or more of these groups.

It is easiest to learn to design borders by working with *one kind of ornamentation* at a time, beginning with simple geometric forms which are repeated or stacked above each other. The form can be repeated so densely that they touch or overlap each other.

Line and surface effect

A drawn border can take on a completely different character if it is done using a wide, flat brush or if certain areas are filled in. Study the picture and see how lines become borders, stripes become squares, zig-zag lines become triangles, and circles become shapes.

If the borders have been colored, it can sometimes be difficult to see what lined pattern was the foundation for the border pattern. Your eye wants to "read together" colors that have the same quality in common — equally light, equally dark, or equally bright. Using different color combinations, you can achieve a completely different effect.

Magic with mirrors

It is like embarking on an adventure when you move two mirrors at an angle of different degrees across a pattern, doodles, letters, or drawings and see the reflection as in a child's kaleidoscope.

These small nature fragments from the borders on page 56 are the foundation for all the borders and mirror image ornamentation on these facing pages.

Mirrors held at 90°, 60°, or 45° angles will repeat the mirrored detail 4, 6, and 8 times respectively. The design above is created by holding the mirrors at a 90° angle. Four small rose-colored leaf forms have been added to fill in the center.

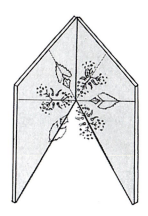

Draw the different angles on transparent paper and keep the mirrors on the paper following the angle you want. Then, pull the paper with the mirrors carefully over the border of the pattern and you will be surprised at how many different results you will get. When you have chosen a design, take the mirrors away and trace off the section you see in the angle. Then, fold the paper following the drawn lines. Since the paper is transparent, you can trace the pattern in the angle the whole way around. This kind of composition is called a central or circle design. A somewhat simplified form will often appear when tracing, but it is important that the lines do not lose their vigor.

After the whole ornament has been drawn, all that remains is to color it in.

When the borders frame rectangular surfaces, the corners have to be taken care of in a satisfactory way. The simplest way is to place a mirror at a 45° angle on the border and then move the mirror back and forth until you find the best symmetrical solution for the corner (see the picture below and on page 95).

The border will be freer and softer if you let it extend around the corner without making it a mirror image. You have to add a few forms to complete the corner (see page 62).

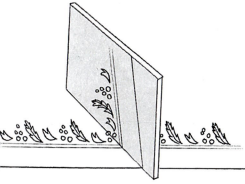

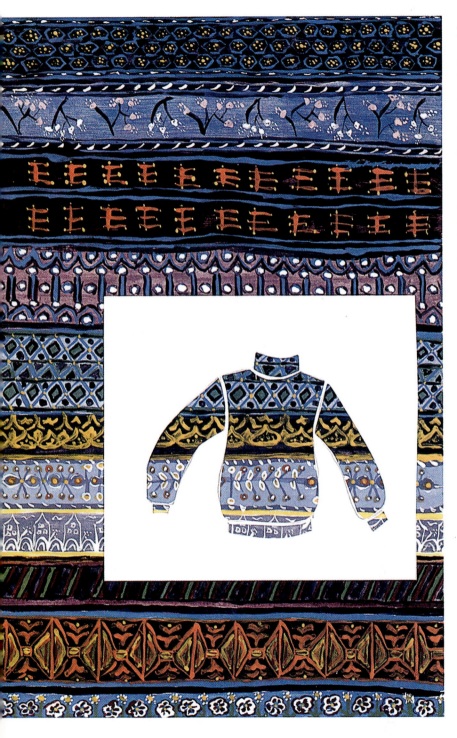

Different sketching methods

Borders can be sketched in many different ways, depending on the desired effect. To avoid small geometric patterns, it is a good idea to sketch with oil pastels which give you rough outlines without detail.

You can draw with crayons on white paper and paint over this with watercolors quickly and with a flowing motion. The watercolors won't adhere to the oily surface, only to the background (sketches 7, 10). You can also color with crayons on an already colored background (sketches 4, 6, 12).

The often bright, clear colors of felt-tip pens can be counteracted by using the pens on rough-surfaced paper and then coloring over lightly with dry crayons, which do not fill in the depressions on the paper (sketches 2, 8). Thin and distinct lines drawn with water-based felt-tip pens can become soft and diffuse if you paint over them with water (see page 70).

Drawn rosepath patterns colored with water colors (sketches 3, 13).

Mixed techniques (sketches 5, 9).

Oil-based pastels on toned down background (sketch 1).

Torn strips of paper painted with water colors; the pattern is colored with pens and opaque color (sketch 11).

Border as surface

The small patterned sketch where the borders cover the whole surface is done in acrylic colors.

Cut out a pattern in the form of a sweater from white paper. The pattern could also be of a mitten, bag, vase or bowl, depending on your handicraft. By sliding the pattern across the borders, you can choose the design which is best suited for the object you are decorating.

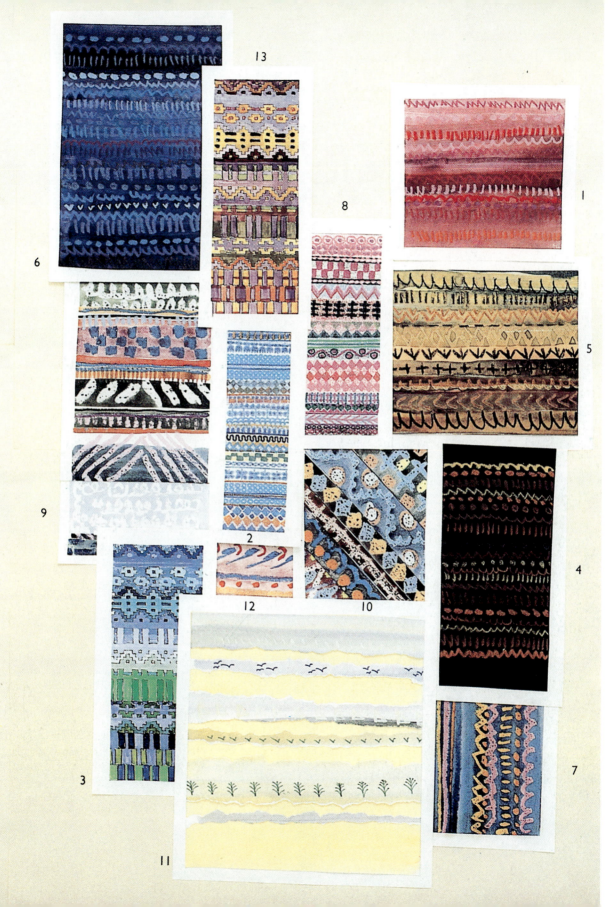

13

8

1

6

5

9

2

4

3

12

10

7

11

Sparsely placed borders

Color many sheets of paper in colors you like. Put aside a few that can be used as background. Cut the remaining sheets into wide and narrow strips and decorate them to your liking. Preferably paint to music.

When you have gathered a number of patterned strips, choose some that go together in color and design and with the background, and arrange them so the surface composition is well-balanced.

In the large picture, borders in light colors have been widely spaced against two different backgrounds. Note how pleasing the narrow solid colored strips are. They tie the surface together, and the transition between border and surface becomes softer. Note how differently the borders appear against the background colors and how small differences can give a different effect to the whole. With a beige background the surface takes on a subdued character, with the pink background, a delicate and playful character.

The borders can extend horizontally, vertically, and circularly. The character of the border can be strengthened with surrounding stripes.

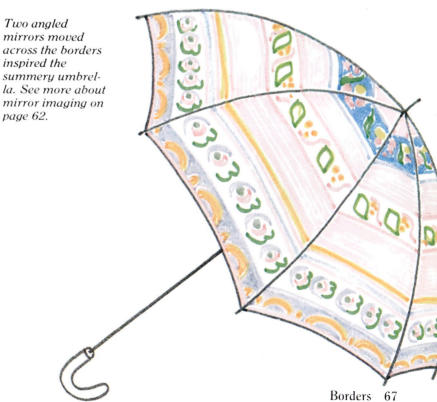

Two angled mirrors moved across the borders inspired the summery umbrella. See more about mirror imaging on page 62.

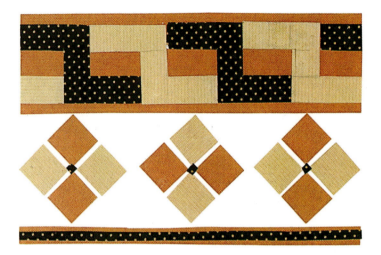

The well-known zig-zag pattern is seen here in three different materials from three different parts of the world.

The clay bowl from Zimbabwe in Africa has been decorated with a border of zig-zags. The inverted triangles are painted black while the triangles between them are decorated with impressions made by a pointed object.

On the root basket from northern-most Sweden, a zig-zag pattern forms an openwork decoration.

The small Russian bowl made of wood has a zig-zag decoration along the rim.

Geometric borders

Look carefully at shopping bags, wrapping paper, and the insides of envelopes before you throw them into the trash. They are often very beautiful, both on the front and the back, and may be used for borders as well as for the ornamentation and background paper.

Practice combining patterned and unpatterned papers by cutting out geometric forms which you will repeat for borders. Make the borders into frames around quotations or greetings.

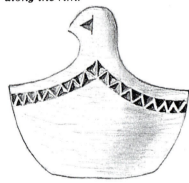

68   Borders

Borders from lettering

The engraved symbols on rune stones form decorative, curving borders. Textiles from the 11th century often have woven or embroidered borders with Islamic, Kufic, or Latin text. The paintings in medieval churches are decorated with "text-borders" with Gothic letters. When we try to create borders with today's alphabet, we are, therefore, following an old tradition.

Draw one or two letters with strong outlines. The letters can also be made with a mirror image so you get symmetrical forms which can be repeated for borders.

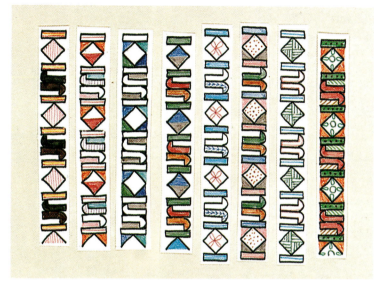

Color variations.

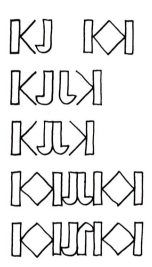

The square design with the star-shaped central figure is derived from the letter-border by using mirror images. The design and the two borders can be seen as one-fourth of the larger area. Place two mirrors at a 90° angle at the center of the star so you can see the whole area.

Play with lines

Let your pen play out soft, winding or straight, broken lines across the paper. It might work best to use water soluble felt-tip markers for this exercise. The sharp line from the felt-tip pen can be blurred with a brush and clean water.

Choose a section which shows movement. Repeat this section at least twice across the paper.

Reverse the designs to make a symmetrical border.

Use your imagination to decorate the color in the border.

Borders with vertical movement.

Accordion cutting

Pleat a wide strip of thin paper into an accordian and cut into it from two, three, or four sides. Unfold the paper and you have a border of regularly repeated pattern formations. If you want the pattern to be even more airy, just refold the paper and cut out more. The pieces that were cut out — the scraps — can be used to enlarge the border (see above).

This cut-out of white paper on a light shaded background can be carried out in wood or plastic as decoration on a gazebo.

Tissue paper cutting

There are many different shades of tissue paper, and since the papers are transparent, you get beautiful color blends when they are pasted on top of each other. For this reason, they can be used advantageously for border exercises.

Fold strips of tissue paper accordion-style and cut into two, three, or four sides. Unfold the strips and choose several whose colors and patterns work together. Paste them so they partially overlap and so the mixed color shows off as a border in itself.

From the cutting in the large picture, you can see that even the white area between the borders has become a decorative element. Tissue paper borders of this kind can be inviting for country-style painting, for example, as a frame around the door or as decoration on an upper door piece.

The borders to the right are suitable for many different techniques — weaving, printing, or even metal work.

The borders in the bottom picture originated from pleated brown packaging paper. The borders, and even the spaces between, are decorated with opaque paint. The brown color of the paper evokes carved and painted decorations on wood.

Here a border has been used as decoration on a glass.

The border in art

The art that the first Egyptians created in their architecture, painting, sculpture, metal work, and textiles is called Coptic. The Coptic textiles, fragments of which have been found in graves from the years 300 to 600 A.D., are some of the oldest and most valuable in history. Borders, squares, ovals, and circles have been woven into these textiles or have been appliqued on top of otherwise unpatterned clothing.

With its mixture of elements from different cultures, it shows the multiple of patterns from the oldest times and it also foretells the development of European medieval art, heraldry, plaited arabesques, animal symbols, and so on.

In architecture, we find borders in friezes, railings, balustrades, and crenelations. The Arm Ebn el As mosque in the oldest section of Cairo is decorated with an open-work crenelation.

The pagoda in the Toschogu shrine in Nikko in Northern Japan is painted and decorated in bright colors on all five stories of the building and gives an overwhelming feeling of borders being stacked on top of borders.

In Poland, borders and flower ornaments are cut out of black △ paper. Additional cutouts in bright colors are used to decorate them.

◁ The Dutch ceramic bowl from about 1920 in the Jugen-style has both geometric and plant motif borders.

Today's borders

Daily we see and come in contact with borders of all kinds; in ribbons, wallpaper, and tiles. But the fringe around the lampshade, the frame around the picture, the lace edging of the cake doily are also borders, even if we are not conscious of them.

Our little town

With potato printing you can get a richly varied surface pattern. Here all the roofs are printed with the same stamp using different colors for each printing. All the houses are the same size. To avoid rigid repetition, three stamps with different cut-outs were used for the windows and doors, which were colored in by hand. By placing the stamps randomly and by not cleaning off the remaining paint between each printing, you will get mixed colors and a liveliness in the pattern which is only possible with hand printing.

An irregular patterned seashell of the mollusk, Conus textile, *which lives in the Indian Ocean.*

A thousand-year-old Peruvian double weave with regular, diagonal pattern.

Patterned surfaces

When a pattern element or ornament is repeated regularly over a surface in both height and width, a surface design or a repeating composition arises. The characteristic of a surface design is that it can be repeated endlessly in all directions. A design is boundless and is built on multiples.

In nature there are many patterned surfaces, but the patterns are always varied and are never repeated exactly. The pattern elements get larger or smaller, denser or sparser, and the colors shift depending on how the patterned surface curves in and out.

Man has many beautiful and skillfully repeated surface designs at his disposal. For many cultures the fear of perfectly repeating patterns has made people "sneak" some little irregularity into the overall design. With this they wanted to show their humility, for "only the Highest can create something complete flawless." The small irregularity could also serve as a hallmark or proof of ownership.

Many surface patterns were derived from the way the process itself makes repetitions. For example, at the loom we can beat out yard after yard of plaid surface pattern, which is built on structure or color effect. At the printing table, we can create surface patterns in freer forms, but the width of the paper or the fabric and the height of the repeat still sets boundary lines for our freedom.

Venetian window from the 15th century with wrought-iron grid as surface pattern, border, and interior of the circle.

From ornaments to surface

One single pattern form does not form a surface pattern, even if its form covers the whole surface.

Two forms next to each other do not become a surface pattern either.

Three or more forms in a row we see as a border or frieze. By placing the forms along the edge of an object, or by clearly defining them above or below with lines, we strengthen the character of the border.

When three or more forms in a row are placed under and above each other, a surface pattern starts to emerge.

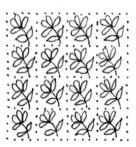

A surface pattern consists of repeated, deliberately placed pattern forms. The dotted lines are used here to make clear the considered placement of the pattern forms and their separation from each other.

The solid lines represent a pattern repeat — the smallest part of the surface which has the total pattern elements in it. Inside this square you can see the distance and placing of the pattern elements in relationship to each other.

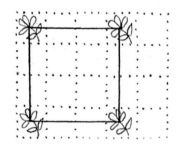

The pattern forms can be shifted in height and width.

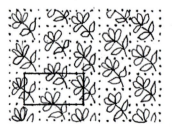

The pattern forms can be alternately turned upside down.

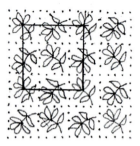

The pattern forms can be done in mirror image.

The pattern forms can be connected two by two. If this is repeated more densely in height than width, you get a surface pattern built up of vertical borders.

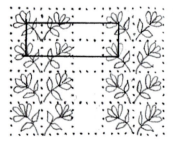

Numerous pattern forms can be connected into blocks which then are repeated a certain distance from each other.

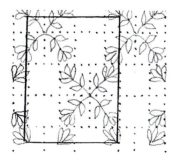

The pattern forms can also be placed so close to each other that they even overlap and it becomes difficult to find a repeat.

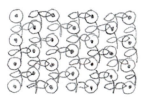

Try to create as many patterns as possible with one single pattern form. You will soon find that variations are almost unlimited, but that it still demands a certain order or a harmony of colors to make the pattern attractive.

You will also find that patterns have different directions. Certain patterns can only be seen from *one* direction. If you try to turn them around, the patterns will seem upside down. We call these patterns *uni-directional* (see page 76).

Uni-directional patterns often have naturalistic or figurative motifs which are naturally placed on vertical surfaces. In textiles they are often called "hanging patterns." Curtains, wallpaper, and fabrics meant for clothing often have uni-directional patterns.

Some other patterns have no direction at all. They can be viewed from all directions. These patterns are called *non-directional*. Splashed wallpaper and small patterned fabrics with dots or spread-out patterns have non-directional patterns. Many geometric patterns are also non-directional, for example, the chessboard (see pages 82 and 83).

Lastly, we have patterns with two or more clearly noticeable directions. These are called *multi-directional*. In textiles we talk about "laying down patterns," since they are often found on horizontal surfaces such as on tablecloths or rugs. Multi-directional patterns often decorate square surfaces such as ceilings, floors, door mirrors, window shutters, gates, and so on. The pattern might originate from the center and radiate upwards, downwards or sideways, or follow the outlines of borders toward the center.

Small designs with a pronounced direction can, when collected four by four, form multi-directional motifs. When many such motifs are put together, they diminish each others' direction and the result is a pattern without direction (see the picture at the top to your left, and the bottom picture on page 90).

There are also some practical things that influence the shaping of the pattern. The size of the repeat depends on the size of the surface that has to be patterned. If the pattern is for wallpaper or fabric for interior decorating or clothing, you have to consider the standard width when manufactured. The width of a repeat has to be evenly divisible by the width of the wallpaper or standard fabric width. The different strips should preferably be designed in such a way that they can be put together with as little waste as possible when matching patterns.

One repeat can, of course, extend across the whole width of the strip, but the height of the repeat depends upon the printing procedure.

When printing with a block, which can be made out of wood, metal, linoleum, cork or potatoes, you can print each block in a specific sequence and location, or completely ignore these and just print to get an attractive surface.

In hand silkscreening, the repeat is restricted to the size of the frame. The frame is not made any larger than you can comfortably reach across by yourself or with a helper.

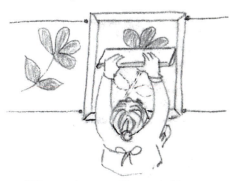

When using a roller-printing machine, the circumference of the roller is the largest possible height of the pattern. A smaller pattern height has to be evenly divided into the circumference of the roller.

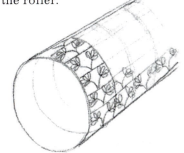

Naturalistic potato print by Jeanne Riss.

Potato printing

The method of cutting out a stamp from a potato cut in half, brushing some paint on it and printing, was brought from France to Sweden by Jeanne Riss, a teacher at Ecole des Arts Decoratifs in Strasbourg. She presented her hand printing method called P-D-T, after the French "pomme de terre" (potato), at an exhibition in Stockholm in May, 1925. The interest in her demonstrations surpassed all expectations, and P-D-T was soon introduced in art classes in many schools.

With potato printing you can quickly and easily repeat a pattern form across a surface. If you twist and turn the stamp, changing the position of the pattern form, you will have a good idea of its possibilities to create and repeat different surface patterns.

When printing a surface pattern, it is easiest to get a good pattern effect if the individual pattern element can be contained in a geometric form, for example: a square, rectangle, triangle, hexagon, circle, etc. Begin by cutting out some forms from black paper. Let the sizes of the forms correspond with each other in some way so the stamps may be combined with each other.

Now make samples for stamps by cutting curved or straight cuts into these geometric forms. By pasting these on white paper, you can easily see which example, when repeated, might create interesting shapes between the forms when joined. Trace this form onto a piece of paper and cut it out. Cut a raw potato in half and cut the pattern form following the paper pattern which is laying on top of the sliced side of the potato. Stroke some color on the raised portion with a brush or use a stamp pad and print on slightly absorbent paper. The stamp can be kept in a plastic bag, but will only last for a few days. For our purposes, a paper plate, paint, and a piece of thin foam rubber make an adequate stamp pad.

Stamp Samples

from a square

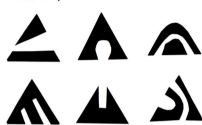

from a triangle

from a circle

Explore all the possibilities of the stamp to form patterns by printing in straight rows, densely or sparsely, or by turning the stamp horizontally or diagonally, or by printing in a circle, or by printing in groups. Try multicolored prints and combinations of different stamps. You can read more about stamp combinations on page 156.

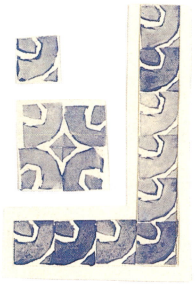

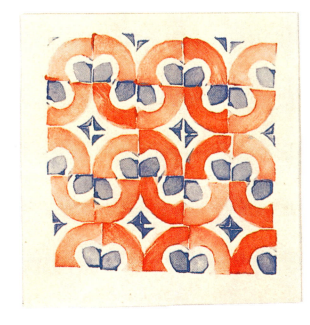
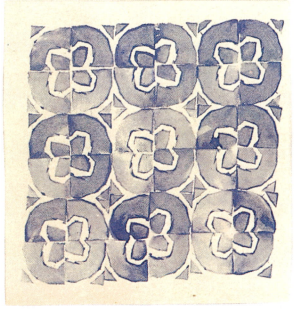

When you repeat a print across the surface, you will soon discover that the spaces between are of great importance. Sometimes the pattern can even be "turned around" so the spaces form patterns against a colored background. We then speak of negative pattern effect as

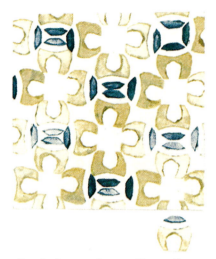

opposed to positive, when the stamp forms the pattern.

If the pattern impression alternates between positive and negative, so you sometimes see

the darker and sometimes the lighter areas, this is called an unstable pattern effect.

By applying the color onto the stamp with a brush, instead of stamping it on a stamp pad, you can put on two or more colors at the same time to get a multi-color print (see picture above).

A surface pattern can be completed by changing color, by condensing, or by making it sparser towards the edges, fading away, and so on, or as on the picture below to the left, by

turning the stamp around in a completely different direction so the pattern changes direction.

Try printing on a patterned background, and also experiment with overprinting. Below is a blue print on yellow-striped background which is overprinted with a small yellow square.

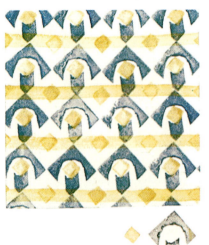

On this and the following page, study how a simple potato print can be developed into a richer pattern design through multicolor printing, printing on a colored or patterned background, overprint, and by a combination of different stamps. Subtle and picturesque printing is developed by printing many times without brushing new color onto the stamp. If you want to print directly onto fabric, then you must use textile paint on the stamp.

Potato prints can be used as shown here for bookcovers and notebooks. The printing can be protected with clear adhesive plastic or can be lacquered for durability.

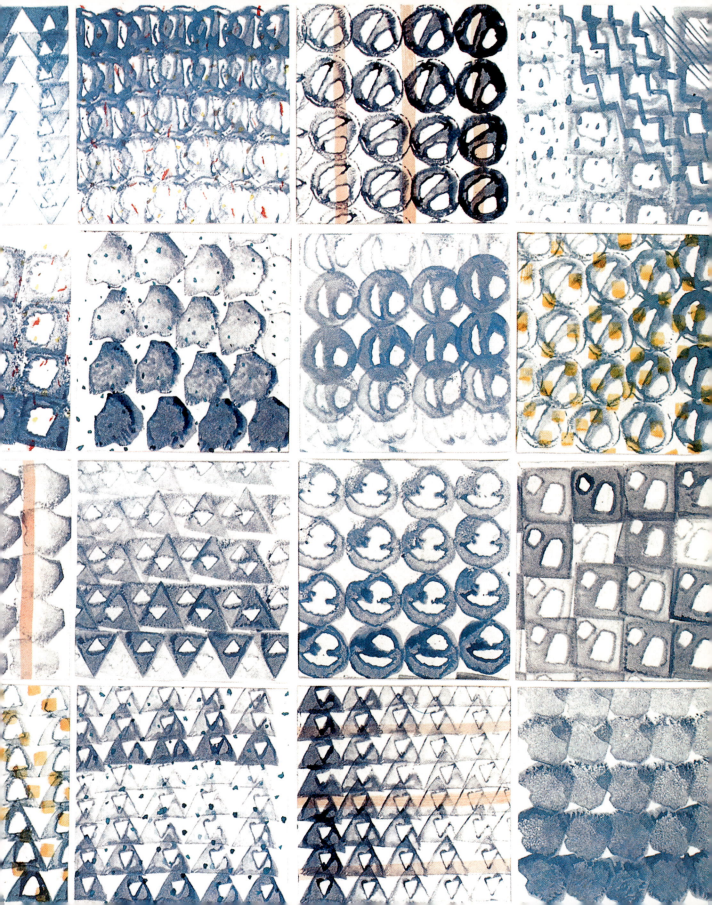

The galloping horses are placed in groups of two, giving the surface design a strong diagonal direction. First an unpatterned animal is printed from each group. By cutting depressions or "dots" from this stamp, you will get a patterned animal.

The sparse surface pattern on black paper is stamped with three different stamps, one of each color. Since the black paper is less absorbent, the color will adhere unevenly, giving a lively and transparent impression.

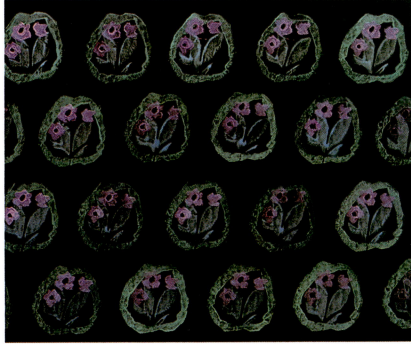

▷ Potato printing can be used advantageously for pictures where many forms build up a motif, such as a leaf design or flower clusters. Here, only a few stamps are used to give the lilac branch depth and life through fading away and over-printing.

Leaf becomes surface

A simple small leaf or flower form can be the source of a multitude of graceful surface patterns. You can use the form exactly as it is, as it stands out against white paper, trace it and then repeat it in different ways for a surface pattern. Be sure the vigor of the lines is retained throughout the pattern. You can, of course, revise the leaf and flower forms first or reduce them to geometric or nonfigurative forms (see pages 102 and 103).

The top row shows an example of two compounded leaf forms which can be seen as a carnation-type flower. Here it has been shaped in different ways, from outlined drawing to colored-in form against a small dotted background. Experiment and try different solutions before you begin working on a surface pattern.

The examples show how the pattern forms can be shifted and slanted in relation to each other in different ways and that different color combinations give a completely different pattern effect. The pattern shows clearly if the light contrast is great, but almost disappears if it is small.

1
Outlines pattern against small patterned background. Sometimes the background pattern might even steal interest from the original pattern.

2
The pattern form is placed in rows with every second form upside down. The horiziontal stripes are counteracted by vertical green stripes.

3
The pattern form is increased with additional leaves and buds.

4, 5
The pattern form is outlined against colored background.

6, 7, 8
Naturalistic forms stand out against a geometric patterned background.

1

2

3

4

5

6   7   8

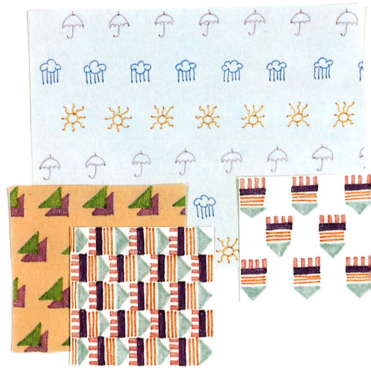

Patterns designed with the help of a grid

Working with a grid preprinted in different simple geometric shapes will greatly simplify pattern making. Lay the sheet under the paper or fabric you are going to paint on. The "square pattern" or grid will show through to serve as a basis for forming the pattern and repeats.

After studying the grid sheets on the opposite page and in "Practical Hints" you will see at once that the patterns at top left have been painted on a triangular grid, the ones on the right on a rectangular grid, and the ones below on a grid of large squares.

Good grid shapes to start with are squares of different sizes, triangles, rectangles or dots.

Begin with a simple grid where the squares are 1 x 1 centimeters (1/3″ x 1/3″). Fill in a pattern form in every square or every other square. A pattern form may be placed and repeated in many different ways: right side up and repeated in straight rows or with every other form turned upside down and every new row shifted

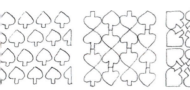

upward in relation to the one before.

Many similar forms can be put together to form a group, which is repeated densely or sparsely across the surface.

The rectangular pattern has many possibilities. One possibility in alternate squares gives a sparse pattern.

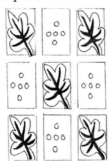

Arabesques can move from square to square.

A motif can stretch through many squares. Here a plant motif ties three rectangles together horizontally. If this form is repeated vertically, a border pattern is formed.

Four reclining rectangles form a base for this geometric pattern where the decorative elements in the spaces between the rectangle pull the composition together. By placing mirrors at an angle at one of the corners, you can see the repeat effect of the pattern.

The dotted pattern gives possibly the greatest freedom for creating patterns. It can inspire flowering vine and wreath patterns, light line patterns, or dense geometric square patterns.

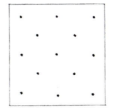

The pictures show how totally different patterns can be derived from one pattern model.

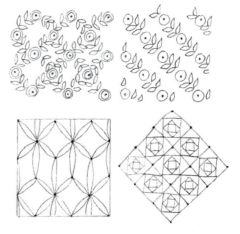

The decoration on both glasses has first been sketched with the help of an underlying grid.

Here the squares of the grid have functioned as an aid in repeating patterns. Also, the lines have been retained as a decorative part of the pattern. Their stiffness is a nice contrast to the soft forms of the nature fragments.

The green pattern has a clear upward direction and is therefore best used for vertical surfaces. Walls, curtains, and fabric for clothing often have patterns with a vertical direction.

The red pattern has no pronounced direction and is therefore suitable for both vertical and horizontal surfaces since it can be seen from all directions without appearing upside down. Parquet and stone floors, rugs, and various decorated table surfaces and tablecloths often have patterns without directions.

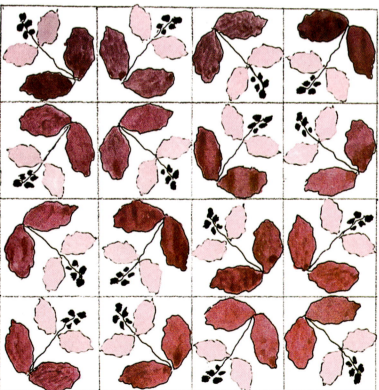

If a fabric is so thin that the underlying grid shows through, then you can draw the pattern directly onto the fabric with textile pens.
The large square grid, with one repeat of the pattern already drawn onto it, is taped to the table. On the grain, guidelines are scratched with a needle horizontally and vertically. As you work, you will move the fabric across the grid horizontally and vertically, until the entire surface is covered.

On the lightweight curtain to the right, the pattern is drawn directly on the fabric with a textile pen. With a simple, painted decoration the mass-produced plastic pot receives a personal touch.

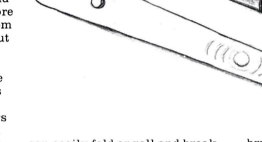

Stenciling

To paint through a template instead of doing it freehand is a technique that has been used in Sweden since the Middle Ages. Then it was used in the churches along with figure painting. Stenciled patterns fill empty areas and form borders along the arches. It was an economical and effective way of copying the more expensive figure paintings. From the end of the Middle Ages, about 1500, and for the next 300 years, stenciling only occasionally appeared in Sweden. During the 19th century this technique was revived as decorations on farmhouse walls. Only 150 years ago handmade wallpaper was a luxury which never reached the farmers. Instead they hired people, who in return for food and lodging, painted directly on the logs or on pasted roll paper.

The principal of stenciling is simple. Cut out the motif which is going to be printed with scissors or knife from a relatively stiff paper or plastic. Then lay the template on top of the material you are going to stencil on and bring the color across the template with a hard brush, roller or dauber. With this stenciling technique you can decorate posters, paper, walls and furniture, or print on fabric.

Making the template

To print a smaller motif you can cut out the template with a hobby knife or a scalpel on a plastic sheet. Always leave ample plastic around the motif. You need one template for each color.

The stencil pattern needs to be simply shaped. Avoid too narrow a distance between forms, "bridges" where the colors can easily run in under the template. Also avoid narrow areas which can easily fold or roll and break with repeated use.

The template can be repaired by putting tape on the broken section on both sides of the template and then cutting out new, clean forms again. Plastic templates may be cleaned in warm water.

When stenciling fabric you can cut out the motifs in self-adhesive clear plastic. The adhesive side of the plastic can adhere to the fabric up to 25 times and prevent the paint from running under the template. When stenciling larger motifs on walls and wallpaper, you can cut out the template in craftpaper and make it durable by shellacking both sides before and after cutting.

The Process

When stenciling, it is very important that the paint be the right consistency. Paint that is too thick will clog small holes in the template easily. Paint that is too thin will run out under the template.

The consistency of the paint, the surface's ability to absorb, and the size of the motif will dictate whether to use a stencil brush, roller, or dauber.

A dauber can easily be made from a round piece of foam rubber. The circle is then filled with small, torn rubber pieces. Make the dauber as firm as possible and tie it tightly.

When stenciling on paper, you can use regular water-based paint carefully diluted with water. When stenciling something which needs to be more durable you can use graphic paint.

When stenciling fabric, the base underneath should be slightly padded. Place a layer of newspaper or a plastic covered blanket under the fabric. Stencil with textile paint and set it with heat. If you are stenciling a sweater, for example, do not forget to put a protective paper *inside* the sweater to prevent the paint from going through to the back of the sweater.

When stenciling paper wallpaper, you will get the best results with primer, which, however, demands a certain experience to work with. Alkyd paint is, on the other hand, easy to use and today most closely compares to primer.

When stenciling, you can achieve more graceful patterns than from potato printing. Here, a flowering Christmas cactus is the basis for the pattern. If the motif only has one color, you will only need to cut out one template. It is important to make the "bridges" wide enough to last through repeated applications of the brush or the dauber.

If you want to work with more than one color, then you must make a template for each color.

With the five templates that have been cut out for this motif, you can work easily. You can redesign the motif for each new stenciling depending on the size of the surface that is to be decorated. Remember to leave space for a Christmas and New Year's greeting next to the stenciling.

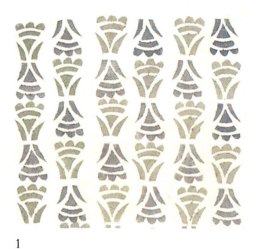

1

2

3

4

5

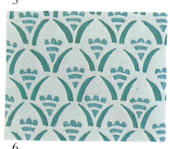

6

7

8

Surface and border

With a stencil you can print large areas relatively quickly, for example, borders and patterns on the walls. If, as in this example, you have a small pattern form which is gong to be repeated onto a small patterned surface, you can cut out numerous forms on the same template. A template made of plastic has many advantages over one of paper. It is easily cleaned and can be used many times. It is transparent, which makes it easier to place the stencils correctly in relation to each other. But, even so, you have to be careful to align the griding marks both on the stencil and the material being stenciled. It is important to place the template correctly both vertically and horizontally and to keep the right distances between the stencils. Be careful not to lay the template on top of a surface which has not yet dried.

For stencils with larger pattern forms, use a template where only every other form is cut out. This permits the pattern to be varied in many ways. You can get a sparsely patterned surface (5), and also a densely patterned surface by stenciling once more in the spaces between. When you stencil in the spaces between, you can change colors and in this way get a more lively pattern effect (1, 2, 4), or you could also turn the template upside down, which in this case gives the surface a striped effect (1).

If you color with a pencil or brush through the template, you can change the colors freely and in this way emphasize completely different details in the pattern (3, 6, 7, 8).

A surface pattern sometimes needs to have an ending. We stated earlier that this can be done by changing colors, by making the pattern denser, by thinning it out towards the edges or by leaving the edges without patterns. The edges can also be made up of borders which mark the end of the surface pattern. The end character of the border is often strengthened with stripes.

Study how the corners have been designed in different ways; more about this on pages 62 and 63.

One of the vault paintings in the Bromma church in Sweden shows how stenciling was used with figure painting during the 15th century. Stenciled motifs fill up all the empty areas and form decorative borders along the arches. The angel is telling Joachim that his wife Anna is going to give birth to Mary, the mother of Jesus. The Latin text in Gothic letters reads in translation: "Hark, I prophesy a great joy for you."

The flock of birds gives an example of how you can get a three-dimensional effect by overlapping the stencil. The group of birds is a picture in itself, but it can also be sparingly repeated for a surface pattern.

If the cut-out figure is undamaged, it can be used as a "turn around" stencil and in this way produce an amusing effect. Place the figure, here a sheep, on a paper and splash or dab paint around the edges to get a "negative" picture to appear. The black sheep is printed in the usual way.

If you print with a relatively dry dauber you will get a charming, soft, uneven surface, which can give depth to the motif. The rough skin of the elephant would be hard to achieve if you worked with a different printing technique.

Stenciled wallpaper from the 1860s. The wallpaper can be found in the Alvrosgarden at Skansen in Stockholm.

Fun to know

One of the oldest known impressions is that of hands on a cave wall in Castillo, Spain, done about 10,000 years ago. The hands stand out as "negative prints." They were done by laying the palm of the hand against the cave wall and then painting around it. The hands are partially covering buffalos painted in yellow and red.

Cottuns

In 1721 a new law forbade using certain objects which could be seen as being detrimentally superfluous. In this so-called superfluity decree, maids and soldiers were forbidden to wear handprinted cotton fabrics, or cottuns (from the English word cotton). Gradually, the women were allowed to use wool and linen fabrics that were woven and printed in Sweden. Small workshops around the country began printing on handwoven fabrics not only on solid colored ones, but also on striped and plaid fabrics. Surprisingly, many women were given permission to print on fabric.

About wallpaper

The oldest preserved wallpaper in Sweden is from the end of the 16th century. The paper was made in sheets and printed by hand. Over time the sheets were pasted together to make them wider before printing. By the end of the 17th century, the printed patterns were also made to match sideways to get a larger overall pattern area. These wallpapers were expensive to make and were reserved for the well-off homesteads. Commoners, farmers, and crafters began painting their log walls. The methods ranged from sprinkling walls with blueberry juice using a birch branch, to creating a simple marble effect by using a bunched-together rag dipped in paint, to intricate stenciling and figure paintings. After 1870 when wallpaper was more common, painting on the walls was forgotten. During the 1970s when many homesteads were renovated, painting the log walls again became popular. Seen through today's eyes, the original wallpaintings far surpass the wallpaper that was later used to cover them. Today, many wallpapers are being printed with old stenciling patterns. Some museums revive old patterns and teach the old handprinting method.

Sketch of a stenciled wallpaper.

About Oriental patterns

Oriental wall decorations and rugs often have patterns of different scales. From far away you only see the large geometric forms. The colors seem to flow together to form a shimmer of color. Oriental design places more importance on color harmony than the shape of the ornamentation. The designer skillfully exploits his knowledge of what colors should be put next to each other so they will blend on your retina. Often a colored area is clearly defined against the

one adjoining it by an outline of a third color.

If the pattern is seen close up you will also discover decorative elements between the large geometric figures. When viewed very closely, you will find that even

these elements are embellished with small patterns.

Surface patterns on spheres

The 1714 Russian church on the island of Kizji in Lake Onega, near the Finnish border, has 22 onion-shaped domes, all of them covered with wooden fish-scale shingles which form surface patterns.

Compare the present surface patterns on the watertowers in Kuwait. The ball-shaped water tanks are also covered with a kind of scales, round plates of enameled sheet-metal in three

different sizes and eleven different colors. The plates are made by Kockums in Sweden and the towers have been designed by Marlene Bjorn.

Are manhole covers museum pieces of the future?

The picture shows a manhole cover in cast iron with a surface pattern done in elevated relief from a street in New York. Millions of coaches, cars, bicycles and shoe soles have passed across this cover and yet have not been able to wear down the pattern more than a fraction of an inch. Maybe in the distant future it will be possible to study these covers at a museum as the only objects remaining from one of the largest cities in the world.

▷

In Japan they combine different surface patterns on the same object with great skill. The patterns have been handed down from generation to generation and are still used on kimonos, pagodas and temples. Today, you can also find the same patterns on all kinds of papers. They wrap gifts with great care and manufacture many objects from this beautiful paper. The well-known Japanese bow is often made up of many narrow strips with different traditional surface patterns.

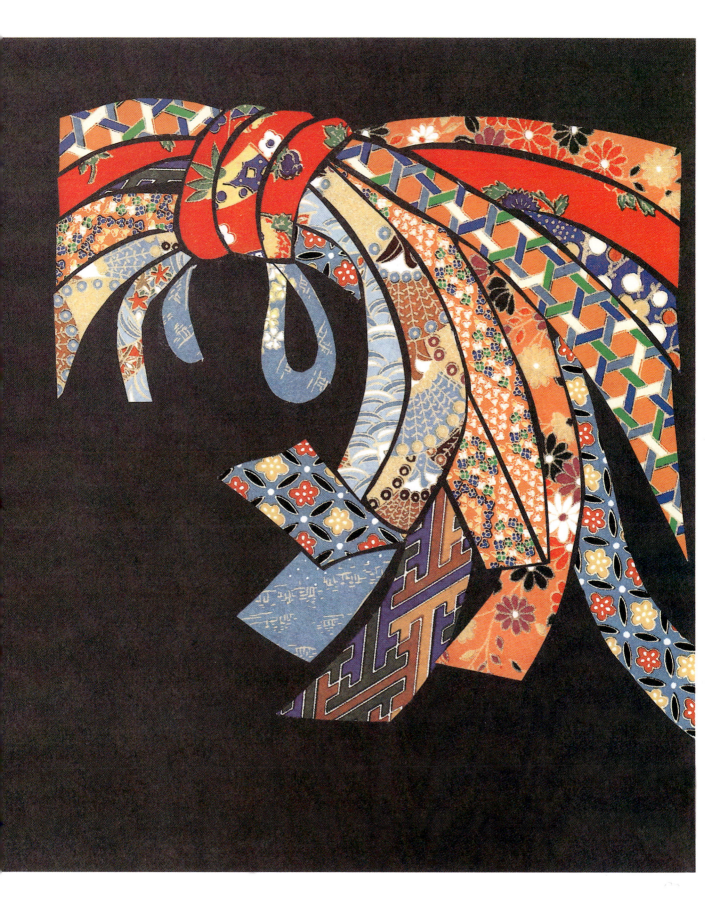

Simplifying

According to the dictionary, the word "simplify" means to make simpler, less complex, easier. In the study of aesthetics, we often use the word simplified instead of naturalistic. When reproducing naturalistically, one imitates as closely as possible the nature of the form, colors, and irregularity. On the other hand, when simplifying, one changes the nature of the form into art forms, which does not imply that only the motif is simplified. As with all artistic works, it requires a conscious effort in redesigning from your source of inspiration an adaptation which simplifies the motif. The simplification can be done in many ways. It can be very close to the natural object or be so far removed that it no longer resembles the original. Simplification can be accomplished if the artist peels away the irregularities and the details so that the only thing remaining is the skeleton of the plants, animals, or objects.

When simplifying you can, for example, emphasize one decorative characteristic at the expense of another, or place greater emphasis on the interplay of lighter and darker areas, or capture the colors of the areas so well that the observer can only guess the form.

Historically, an original naturalistic form — a tree, flower, or animal — has been reproduced so often that it has become more and more simplified, but still retains its principal characteristics. Some designs have in this way kept their character through hundreds of years; on the other hand, over the years, some have been so altered and reshaped that only an expert can trace the prototype.

The way simplification has been done, and is being done, is dependent on the artist's intention and the material with which he is working. Difficult and coarse materials lend to further simplification. The manner of simplification varies from culture to culture, and from one period to another. Consequently, we can talk about a personal, national, or historical style. What they all have in common is that they release the accidental occurrences of nature and transform them into art forms.

The simplest way of stylizing, for example, a flower or plant, is to draw it as viewed from the top or from the side. Sometimes, the flower as seen from beneath or in a cross section might present a decorative form.

The cut-out exercise on the opposite page gives a sample of how a nature study can be stylized in different ways. Paint or draw a cross-section of a piece of fruit — fruit often has decorative seedpods. Trace the outlines onto black paper (see page 156) and cut out the fruit and the seedpod. Work alternately with black and white backgrounds to get positive and negative pictures. Try different shapes, simplifications, and variations of the motif. Thin and narrow details can be painted or drawn.

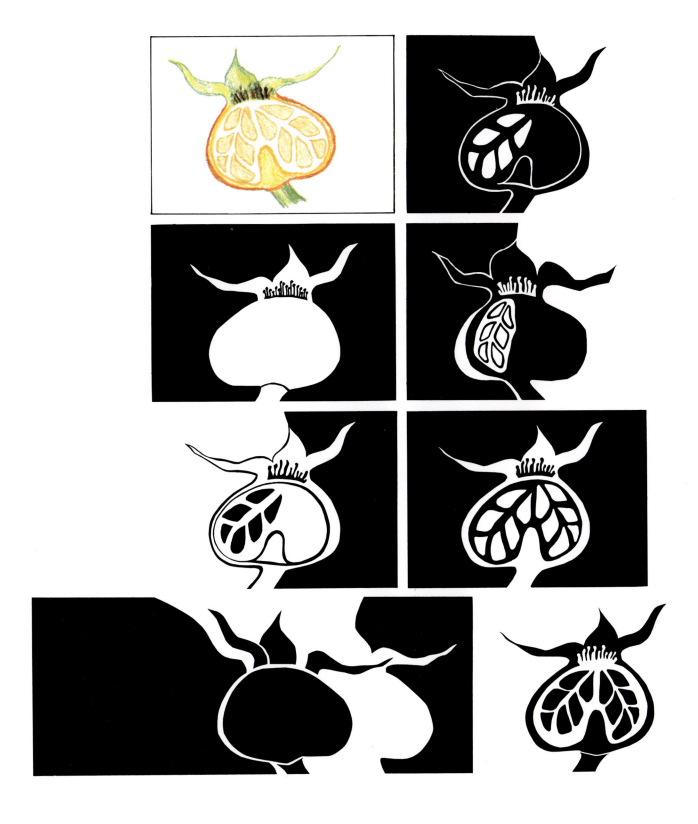

Simplified form as ornament and surface pattern

This exercise shows how a form can be reworked into different kinds of surface patterns.

Rosehips from the previous exercise have been used as starting material. An outline of a rosehip is enticing for its shape. It can be repeated densely or sparsely in a surface pattern. Many similar rosehips can also be collected into a group and in this way form a larger design which, in its turn, can be arranged to form new patterns. The pattern with four such groups brought together forms a cross shape which suggests church ornamentation.

◁ Retrace the outlined pattern on colored paper. Color in the patterns. It is harder than you may think to find colors which stand out effectively against a given background.

Eight rosehips together make a larger flower formation. Many such flower formations have been reduced with a copy machine. Sometimes it might be fun to use this technique with multifolding, enlarging, or reducing a form. Then cut, paste and regroup into patterns with different characteristics. Here it has become an airy surface pattern. The sepals of the rosehip form graceful circles, while the rosehip groups stand out as darker crosses.

In this exercise the rosehips have been connected in a slightly different way and four dark leaf forms have been added which give the surface pattern greater contrast between light and dark sections.

Simplifying by cutting, tearing and folding out

Sometimes it is useful and instructive to work with surfaces instead of with lines. Drawing produces lines; cutting produces surfaces. In these simplifying exercises, try to cut out or tear the motifs from paper. This method also automatically simplifies the motif.
(See the bull below.)

Many handicraft techniques are based on either the decorative combination of the surface and the surrounding spaces, or the contrast between the rough and shiny surfaces of relief work. To try these techniques you can sketch on a slightly-tinted paper, such as ragpaper.

Cut-out in shaded paper

Cut or tear out the motif and think about where it might be natural and decorative to make additional cuts to divide it into smaller pieces. Pull the pieces apart and shift them in relation to each other so spaces are formed between the pieces. These spaces will enliven the larger area and

fill it with a rhythmic lineplay. Don't throw away the pieces that are left over from both sides of the motif. Placed away from the motif they can form an effective frame (see also page 101).

The method of cutting and pulling apart can be combined with the method of cutting and unfolding. Make soft curved cuts across a sheet of paper. Pull apart the pieces and make cuts into the outlines. Fold the cut-outs to the spaces in between and shift all pieces until a harmonious combination appears between positive and negative spaces.

Exciting pictures from a few cuts

With only five cuts from side to side on a long, narrow piece of paper you can get a rich pattern of budding branches. Experiment with the spaces between the pieces. Although this sampling technique is meant for handicrafts which are based on textural effect rather than color effect, it might be fun to color and decorate the sample in different ways and find completely new areas of use.

Why not add color with the help of colored pages from magazines, fashion journals, or travel brochures? First trace the original sketch onto transparent paper. Bring this sketch across the magazine pictures and look for the right sized color surfaces for the different pieces. You will soon find that the shapes of the pieces will not tolerate areas of color which are too "busy."

If you like, you could make your sketch a little more elegant by using gold paper or a pen with gold ink.

Cut-out in white paper

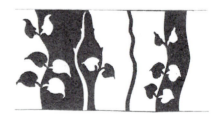

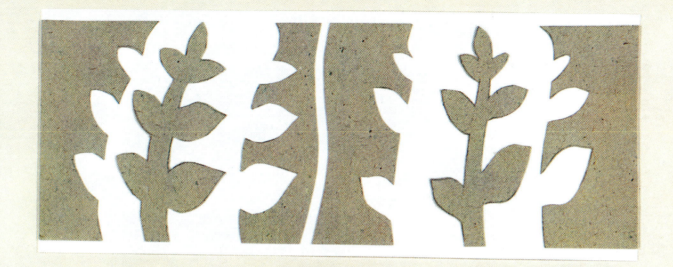

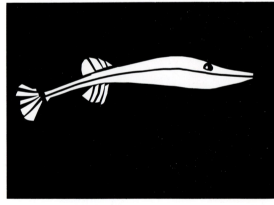

Simplifying and decorating fish

The inspiration for this exercise can be found in one of the many books about the 20,000 fish in the world. Visits to aquariums and zoological shops might also inspire you to work with unusual forms.

Study "your" fish to find its decorative forms and color changes. Draw the outlines of the fish, and its fins, gills and eyes. Don't forget that dots, color stripes, and squares also might have decorative input.

Transfer the drawing onto stiff white or black paper and cut out the silhouette. Cut on all the drawn lines and pull apart the pieces. Try to completely eliminate certain areas so you can later fill them in with decorative elements.

Color the fish, too. The design might be used as a print on a beach bag or enlarged and executed in metal and colored glass as a sign for a fish shop; or in dramatically reduced scale as a piece of jewelry.

Decorating animal figures is nothing new. Just look at the Egyptian hippopotamus in clay made about 2000 B.C. It is decorated with stylized lotus blossoms and water-lily pads, plants from the natural habitat of the hippopotamus. The small Chinese deer from the end of the 15th century is adorned with gold-outlined enamel inlay in the form of white flowers.

The dried fish are seashore finds. The small fish has been swimming in waters far from the Swedish coast, but the larger one was found on Oland.

Exercise with limited color scale in three degrees of value

In many techniques, a strong simplification and limited color scale is advantageous. In this exercise, you simplify by emphasizing the difference in light between different areas. The colors are limited to two, one color in three degrees of value.

In the window motif you can clearly observe the contrast of the degrees in light between inside and outdoors. Sketch a window, preferably at the breakfast table, to include some typical, everyday objects. Then limit the picture so that only important forms are included. Determine what color scale you want to use and where you would use three to four values of the same color plus one contrasting color. Study which areas should be dark and which areas should be light. Color in the sketch to see if you have emphasized the right areas before you execute the motif in a print, or as in this example, an appliqued picture.

"And is the fern less decorative than the leaf of the acanthus? Why not use the leaf arabesque of the maple for a pattern for a wall surface . . . The daisy, the bachelor's button, the water-lily and the water-lily pad — all of them grow outside our own yard, excellent in form and color, and are just waiting to be severely stylized and elevated to decorative duty."
Verner von Heidenstam

Decorate a given form

The Cuna Indians on the San Blas Islands located off the coast of Panama in the Caribbean produce some of the most sought-after handicrafts of modern times. Their work, the rectangular fronts and backs on women's blouses, which are called Molas, is sewn in a reversed applique and are in great demand by collectors all over the world.

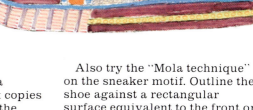

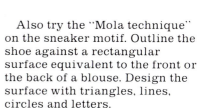

Draw a picture of some common object. Why not a sneaker? Make five or six copies of this outlined shoe. Fill the surfaces with patterns in gay colors, luxuriously, and at random. Play and have fun!

Also try the "Mola technique" on the sneaker motif. Outline the shoe against a rectangular surface equivalent to the front or the back of a blouse. Design the surface with triangles, lines, circles and letters.

A Mola can be made of up to five layers of different bright colors. You cut down through layer after layer of fabric and then hem-stitch each color tightly and neatly to the layer below. A Mola is considered to be of high quality if all lines are of equal width and no area is without a pattern. The original patterns were geometric and abstract. Today you can see how they are inspired by advertising, stamps, cigarette advertising, political pictures, the Crucifixion, or Noah's Ark. Yes, even a Swedish matchbox cover has inspired a Mola seamstress. The Cuna Indians are illiterate, and for that reason letters are decorative elements only.

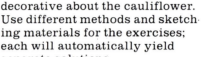

Exercise with cauliflower

Study the motif, here a cauliflower, by drawing it with pencil or ink, or paint it with watercolors freehand. Try to find out what is characteristic and decorative about the cauliflower. Use different methods and sketching materials for the exercises; each will automatically yield separate solutions.

Felt tip pens invite line drawing. The drawing can then be softened by painting across it with brush and water.

One further step to simplifying is to transfer the drawn outline of the study onto black paper (see page 156) and cut out the form. This silhouette is in itself a simplification. The silhouette can be lightened with cut-outs which emphasize the character and enrich the motif.

Take some of the black/white cut-outs as a basis for further imaginative interpretations of the cauliflower. Collect "colors" from pictures in magazines for the exercises. Generously use completely alien colors for the cauliflower when you cut, paste, fold, or make collages. Try to work against a colored background.

Begin the collage exercise by making an outline of the cauliflower on colored paper. Fill the form either completely or partially with torn or cut pieces from your "color collection." It is freer, but also harder, to build up the collage completely without a base drawing.

The collage can also be done with tissue paper. It is a good idea to tear thin paper. If you then fasten the pieces lightly at the center only, the free, torn edges will help to underline the character of the cauliflower. The colors hold together when the pale colored background shows through the thin tissue paper.

Simplifying with tissue paper

As we mentioned earlier, simplifying can be done in many different ways. It can be quite faithful to the original or so far removed that you would not recognize the model. You can simplify by cultivating the form or by only pointing out the colored areas or the degrees in the color intensity. In the example of the geranium, the first one is close to the natural, despite the "incorrect" color scale and the fact that all the surfaces have been torn and cut freehand. Because the tissue paper is transparent, it will form darker shades when many layers of the same color are pasted on top of each other. Where different colored papers overlap, soft blended colors are formed. After the paste has dried, a simple outline drawing on the layered tissue paper will strengthen the flower's character.

The next two pictures show how, by looking at a small area of the picture, you will get new surfaces and exciting lineplays. These new pictures can then be used as a sketch for tapestry weaving or silk-screening or even glass painting.

On the picture on the opposite page, the geranium has been changed to a surface pattern using the same technique of torn and cut tissue paper pasted with wallpaper paste. The pattern done with transparent tissue paper is reminiscent of printing done on light silk or velvet.

Stylized birds

Rapphen, silk embroidery in chain stitch, Altai, Siberia, about 400 B.C.

North American Indian decorations on clay pots and leather.

Painting from a 20th century Polish ceramic plate.

Weaving and embroidery pattern known worldwide.

Paper cut-out, 20th century Poland.

Fresco-painting from an ancient Persian weaving, Turkestan, 600 B.C.

Designing with pipe cleaners

Designing with pipe cleaners or thin wires may be unfamiliar to many and the material may feel strange at the beginning. But you will soon be captivated by its shaping possibilities. The thickness and length (1 m or approximately 39″) of the pipe cleaners will let you form the figures in a continuous line, which will give you soft simplified forms. Long pipe cleaners are perfect for group work where each person can form his own animal or flower which then can be joined together with those of the other participants (see page 153). The line-pattern that appears can be traced, enlarged, colored, and decorated. Here the task was to form a gate for a zoo. You may also choose to make a gate for a playground, botanic garden, circus or sports field (see page 156).

Also try to design a motif in a geometric form in such a way that the motif fills up the surface by touching the borders in many places. There are unlimited possibilities to convert the patterns you get from this method of sketching using different materials and techniques, such as patterns for quilting or forging. On a reduced scale, it might inspire jewelry making or enamel work.

FOOTNOTE: Pipe cleaners of this length may not be readily available in all areas.

Many old houses from the beginning of this century had decorations in soft, elegant Jugendstil. The sketch shows a lead inlaid Jugendstil window with the flowers and winding ornaments typical of the style.

Picture-symbol
Letter-picture

In the beginning man drew pictures, which slowly became simplified symbols and then became letters. Today we seem once again to be returning to the picture. The picture language is becoming popular all over the world and we strive to make the pictures as simplified and general as possible so they can be read and understood in most cultures.

Twenty-thousand years before Christ, people were carving and painting pictures on the walls of caves where they lived. Most pictures in those days were of the hunted game such as the buffalo, wild horses, and deer. People were never pictured except for their handprints. Not till thousands of years later were figures of people found, often simplified to stick-figures with their animals. As lifestyles became more and more varied and complicated, so did our pictures. Man then discovered how to communicate with others by hieroglyphics, which were different from cave paintings since their message was communicated step-by-step in a series of pictures. The pictures were done with as few lines as possible and they proceeded to become symbols. These, in turn,

evolved slowly in different ways into letters. Today we are back to picture language.

The Horus falcon, here painted on papyrus with hieroglyphics on the side, represents the old Egyptian way of communicating.

The hieroglyphics are interpreted from top to bottom as a linen braid, face, mouth, baby bird.

In Scandinavia there are picture stones and rune stones where the hard, carved stone give both script and picture a simple formation. The figures on the stones and rocks are greatly simplified. Without the carved, cut and gaudily painted picture stones from Gotland, we would have hardly any knowledge of the last 700 years of our prehistoric age. On the picture stones we can study the rigging and crew of Viking ships. The squares on the sails are actually plaited together from narrow strips making them

strong. If the strips were of contrasting colors, you would see a showy checkered pattern.

At the top of the picture stone from the 8th century from Huminge in Klinte on Gotland, you can see a rider on his way to Valhalla, a welcoming valkyrie, two fighting men, and a ring or

wreath carrier. Underneath that, a ship is steering across furious waves, and at the bottom stands a farm with a tethered cow, a gabled house, and three archers.

The stamp shows a Viking ship from the Larbro stone, originally

from Stora Hammars on Gotland. It is kept at Bunge National History Museum close to Farosund.

Today's symbols and pictographs

Symbol has so many meanings today that we will call on the Danish author Sven Tito Achen for help in explaining the concepts. In his book *Symbols Around Us* he gives the definition of the word symbol as follows: "A symbol is a figure or picture which represents an object but means something else."

Male	Female	Drugstore
Mars	Venus	(a snake that is dripping
Iron	Copper	its venom into a bowl)

Even if the symbol is simple, it can only be understood by the initiated. Neither logic nor common sense suffice to learn its meaning. Its meaning has been arbitrarily decided.

St. John's cross as a symbol for place of interest.

Pictography has become our period's picture language, especially in international connections when applied to traffic and communications, tourism, the Olympic games, washing instructions, and so on.

A pictograph is a picture that means what it represents. If a picture of a fish means a fish shop, then it is a pictograph. If it means "I am a Christian," then it is a symbol.

For hundreds of years, shop-keepers all over the world have been hanging simplified pictures,

so-called pictographs, outside their shops. In addition to telling the shopper what products and services are being offered, they also serve as guides for the tourist who does not know the language of the country. The picture of a pretzel or scissors and comb or a pair of eyeglasses can be understood by everyone.

If you stroll through the small, idyllic town of Mariefred in

Sweden, you will find many new signs on the streets and around the market place made in the old-fashioned way. Besides serving a practical purpose, they contribute to the quaint atmosphere among the low, wooden houses of yellow, blue, pink, and green with white trim and carefully tended flowerboxes.

Attributes are symbolic objects which in the pictorial art world occur in connection with gods, saints, and biblical figures — Neptune's trident, Saint Peter's keys, and the seashell of the pilgrims, without which we would not know who is who.

Pictograms used as warnings or information

Wild animals	Slippery when wet
ferry station	Hostel
Lockers	Hand wash
Access for the handicapped	Restaurant

Sports pictograms for the Olympic Games, Munich, 1972.

Soccer	Swimming
Weightlifting	Rowing
Boxing	Basketball

Pictograms used in daily newspaper announcements.

Boats	Business transaction
Education	Vocational and handicraft help

Color studies
for practical use

Every day thousands of colors flow toward us — colors which give us stimulation and happiness and which have become such natural elements in our lives that we have a hard time imagining an existence without them. We have also become more aware of how much the color in our surroundings influences us, that color is not just an aesthetic issue, but that it also has an effect on our well-being. For example, our heartbeat will increase in a red room; in a blue room we will miscalculate the time. Too dark ceilings oppress us, and too light floors will make our steps uncertain. We know that bright, clear colors one day will make us exhilarated and happy, while the same colors on a different day and in a different mood might make us tired, irritated, or distracted. We also are constantly exposed to new color combinations in fashion and interior decorating. What might not have worked yesterday may feel natural and right today. Many people insensitively and carelessly combine colors which may be physically painful and irritating in the same way as off-key notes are painful to the musical person.

Researchers say that people's color sense has developed during past centuries. *The Illiad* and *The Odyssey,* for example, describe an almost colorless world. The Bible often mentions the sky, but never describes it as blue. In cultures where colors don't play a practical role there are no words for them either; you are hardly conscious that they exist. There are so called two-color cultures, which only have words for black and white. In three-color cultures, the third color is always red, and in four-color cultures the fourth color is yellow.

The color study

- teaches us to organize colors into groups depending on their different qualities,
- shows us how colors influence each other,
- trains us to be sensitive to color,
- gives us a common color language.

Do we need to study color?

Yes. Look at all the color samples on the next page. You will *see* that all the colors are different, but you might be surprised at how few of them you can *describe* in words.

A person's eye can comprehend a hundred thousand shades of color. From these we can separate six colors with independent color character. They are clear yellow, clear red, clear blue, clear green, white and black. They are called *primary colors.* All the other colors resemble these. Now look at the samples once more and then try to describe their relationship to one or more of the primary colors.

Wherever you combine a few of these by chance (red, blue, green and yellow colors), you will get exciting color compositions from which to continue working.

Gray scale or value of shades of light

White and black and all gray shades in between are called color values. These values can be organized in a scale from white (the lightest color value) across gray to black (the darkest color value). This scale is called the gray scale or value of shades of light.

◁ *Since the eye is very sensitive to the differences among shades of gray, it is both fun and easy to make your own gray scale from pieces of torn black and white newspaper pictures. This "scale" will often be surprisingly beautiful. Note that the "window frames" on the picture seem darker where the background is lighter and lighter where the background is dark.*

The value of a color is read by comparing it with the gray scale. Where the difference between the color and the noncolor of the gray scale is the least, the value is the most similar. We say that colors with the same amount of light reflection on the gray scale have the same value. (See more about this on page 129).

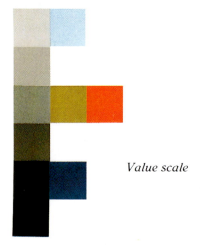

Value scale

How pink is the pig?

Everybody with normal color vision sees the color the same way, but the way each person perceives the same color varies from person to person. We also feel differently about colors depending on interests, temperaments, cultural background, and experiences. This makes it hard for us to unambiguously describe our color impressions to each other. Often we compare one color with the color of some *object* familiar to all. We might say that a sweater is tomato red, but the tomato can have different degrees of ripeness and consequently, different red colors. And nobody knows exactly which shade of red you associate with the tomato. On the color scales here, you can see how a group of nine persons get nine different suggestions on how sky-blue, pig-pink, forest-green and snuff-brown looks. If we use *fancy names* such as shocking pink, baby blue, or hunter green as a description of a color, the confusion grows. It is better to use the crayon names on colors — ultramarine, carmine, cinnabar, umber, and so on. They are *ingredient names;* names of the chemical substances which have been used when manufacturing the actual color substances. For exact color description, these names are also unsatisfactory since one and the same color substance can be found in many different manufacturing processes. Carmine, for example, can look different depending on its manufacturer.

The number of clearly descriptive words for colors is very limited. Simple, *uncombined color names* are yellow, red, blue, green, white, black, gray, and possibly orange and violet. These color names can be combined to form yellow-red, red-blue, which in turn can be additionally made clearer by using light or dark, soft or bold, clear or unclear — but each description still contains a multitude of variations.

121

Colors and things awaken our imagination

Crystal white, glacier white, pearl white, frost linen, snow crust and meringue white.

Wheat, gray haze, sand gray, oat beige, seaweed and natural linen.

Gladvine, mustard rose, honey rose, caramel, raspberry and cloudberry and cerise.

Bark brown, seaweed, black pepper, stone brown, brown-black and Havana.

Opera red, antique purple, revolutionary red, warm red, Emma pink and maraschino cherry.

Intense blue, lustre blue, sargasso blue, phosphorus blue, azure blue and swimming pool blue.

Thistle purple, violet lustre, litania, grandmother's purple, Aunt Purple and boudoir purple.

Spring scent, dictionary green, pistachio, mignonette, seagrass and prairie grass.

Bankers' gray, ash gray, dapple gray, night gray, cave gray and blacktop gray.

Colors have different characters

Artists, writers, and researchers have documented and even developed theories about how we psychologically, aesthetically, and emotionally experience and are influenced by colors.

Colors and things awaken our imagination

◁ *When the eye is attracted to a color on a surface as well as its texture, then the visual and the tactile combine to stimulate our imagination. Often, when describing a color, we want to evoke the surface as shiny or dull, rough or smooth, complicated or simple.*

In many fields we use fantasy names for colors. In the fashion industry, for example, the name of a color used in advertising will give us pleasant associations, in the direction desired by the sponsor. Try it yourself, free your imagination and put enticing, seductive, poetic or humorous names on colored things of many different kinds.

Pastel colors are often seen in Scandinavia as sweet, shimmering, and ethereal while the same colors in the intense light of more southern latitudes are seen as faded and gray.

◁ *Bright-colored, clear and pleasing colors,* so-called saturated colors, we think of as lively, but also as loud and glaring. Those in different latitudes with stronger sunlight seem to crave more saturated colors.

Oversatisfying, clear colors we see as deep and sonorous. Simply stated, you can say that saturated colors with black added are called oversatisfying, and saturated colors with white added are unsatisfying.

Dark, dull colors we think of as being rich earth tones.

Average light, weak color, and neutral gray we find as calm and quiet, but maybe also seem boring and flat.

During the rococco period of the 18th century, gray and pastel colors were cherished in furniture and interior decoration. During the second half of the 19th century, strong, intense colors predominated. The Jugend-style at the turn of the century used light colors, and from the 1930s on we get the Funkis-period's white walls. Periods with light, soft colors rhythmically seem to alternate with periods of strong colors.

Arranging colors

By arranging colors systematically we gradually get a certain overview of all the colors. Begin by arranging strong, clear, saturated colors into a scale where one color overlaps the next and where the end of one scale is the beginning of the next. Arrange the six colors — yellow, red, blue, green, white, and black — with independent color character as a starting point.

Begin with clear yellow. The yellow becomes yellow-orange, orange, red-orange to clear red. The red goes from more bluish-red color through violet to clear blue. The blue goes from blue-green colors to clear green, and the green goes from yellowish-green shades to clear yellow. These four scales are brought together into a color circle also called a color spectrum. The circle is usually made up of 16 traditional colors, which is enough for practical purposes.

The scales between white and black are found on page 120.

Color dragon

Playfully organize yarn pom-poms, ribbons, or fabric pieces following the plan on the opposite page and make an undulating color dragon. When the dragon can bite its own tail you will have a color circle.

Color circle with flowers

You can also cut and paint flowers for a color circle. For each flower you will need two square papers; one 15 x 15 centimeters (6" x 6") and the other one 12 x 12 centimeters (4¾" x 4¾"). Fold the papers in half as many times as you wish and cut from the outer edges, so that when the paper is unfolded it will look like a flower. Paint both papers in the same color. If this exercise is done in groups, then the first group should paint its two flower forms in clear yellow, the second should use yellow-orange, the third orange, and so on, around the whole circle. Pin up the double flowers forming a wreath against a white or black background. The more flowers you paint, the more luxuriant the wreath will become.

The natural color system

The Swedish color system, which has acquired the name "natural color system or NCS," originates from the way we see colors for their quality and their interrelationships. NCS is built of six clear colors, the primary colors: Yellow, red, blue, green, white and black, which can be determined with the help of our inborn color perception. Every color can vary depending on value (brightness of the color), plus the addition of white and black.

The primary colors are abbreviated in the following way:

- Y = yellow
- R = red
- B = blue
- G = green
- W = white
- K = black

To illustrate this system we use three geometric figures; the circle, the triangle, and the doublecone or the colorbody.

The color circle. The colors, usually exemplified by 16 color hues in their maximal brightness or saturation, are reproduced in a color circle. The four "clear" primary colors are placed as the four cardinal points on a compass with yellow in "north," red in "east," blue in "south," and green in "west." The primary colors divide the circle into four

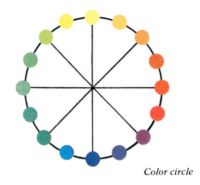

Color circle

quadrants; one yellow-red I, one red-blue II, one blue-green III, and one green-yellow IV. Each color in a quadrant shows its relationship to the adjacent

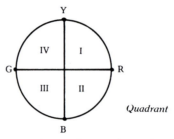

Quadrant

primary colors. The quality of the primary color that appears the strongest is called its main-tendency, the weaker one is called its bi-tendency. The color which lies between two primary colors, and which is as much related to one as to the other, is called center color and divides each quadrant into two octants. Orange, violet, blue-green, and yellow-green are center colors.

The color triangle. The hue of the color, the so-called degree of

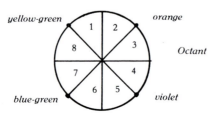

Octant

the color (color strength), the hue (black added), and the tint (white added) are reproduced in an equilateral triangle which is defined by three scales: white (W) to black (K), the so-called gray scale, black to maximum color (C), and color maximum to white.

The colors are organized so that the tint (or amount of white) increases towards W, the color intensity increases towards C, and the shade (or amount of black) increases towards K. The color with equal amounts of black, intensity, and white ends up in the center of the triangle. Every color in the color circle, or wheel, has its own color triangle.

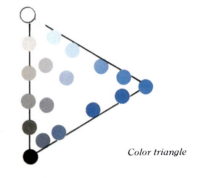

Color triangle

To describe a color, you have to use both the color circle and the color triangle (see also page 156).

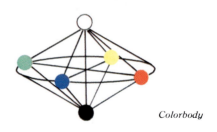

Colorbody

The doublecone or color body. All color triangles can be thought of as assembled into a three-dimensional figure, the color body which looks like a double-cone, with the gray scale from W to K as a common center axis. In the center of the doublecone you will find the color circle, which is formed by the color triangles of the highly saturated hues. In the color body, each color is in a position to be compared in relationship to every other color.

The gray scale. The intensity of the colors, which is not the same as their whiteness, is read in comparison to the gray scale. Read more about this on pages 120 and 129.

The greatest benefit of the NCS-system is this: If you wish to unambiguously characterize a color, its strength, whiteness (tint), and blackness (shade), you can use the letter and number codes of the NCS-system for reference.

Each quadrant in the color circle is divided into 100 sectors and every tenth step is marked on the periphery with letter and number combinations. Y identi-

fies a color which is 100% clear yellow. Y10R identifies a yellow color with 10% red and 90% yellow. The red rises by 10% for each step on the circle to Y90R, which means the color is almost completely red; it has 90% red and 10% yellow.

The numerals in the yellow-red quadrant give the amount of red, the numbers in the red-blue quadrant the amount of blue, the numbers in the blue-green quadrant the amount of green, and the numbers in the green-yellow, the amount of yellow.

Color triangle

The color triangle is divided in a similar way into tenths with one set of lines parallel with W to K scale line and another parallel to the W to C scale line. All the colors along the K-10 line have 10% black, along the K-70 line, 70% black. The colors along the C-60 line have 60% intensity.

The sum of black, intensity, and white has to be 100%. When the amount of black and the color are expressed in percentages, the remainder is the amount of white and, therefore, does not need to be indicated.

A color is described in the following order: amount of black, intensity, and amount of white. 2060-R90B indicates a blue-red color with 90% blue and 10% red. It has 20% black, 60% intensity, and 20% white. In this way the 1412 color samples in the NCS-color atlas can be described exactly.

NCS-circle

We like to describe the brightly-colored leaves as yellow-green, dark green, light yellow, bright red or rust brown, depending on the time of the year.

Warm and cool colors

By interpreting colors in different ways, colors can, as we have said before, evoke different moods. For example, we feel that some colors are cool, others warm. Warm colors are generally thought of as being in the yellow-red area and cool colors in the blue-green area, but there are contrary opinions whether it is the weak blue color or the strong blue color which gives the coolest feeling.

Cool colors

Greeks definitely do not feel that blue is cool. Whether a color is seen as cool or warm depends also to a large extent on the surrounding colors. Here you can see, for example, how the reddish-brown strip looks cool next to the yellow and how it takes on a warmer tone when it is put with blue.

We also talk about warm and cool shades of green. The yellowish-green is seen as warm compared to the bluish-green,

Warm colors

but cool compared to the reddish-yellow.

In the same way, you can talk about warm and cool reds and warm and cool yellows and blues. Warmth usually increases with color-strength, except with the whitened and grayed colors where even very weak hues can be warm. It is only by comparing one color to another that you can decide if it is warm or cool, light or dark.

Warm color character is usually strengthened by soft, fuzzy forms and wooly, coarse textures. Cool color character is usually strengthened by rugged and sharp forms and by hard, shiny surfaces.

Cool and warm colors in an optic mixture create vibrations, life, and light in a picture. Optic mixtures arise when small dots or lines are placed next to each other on the surface, and only from a distance are seen to blend. In the art world, this is called pointillism.

Active and passive colors

We can also experience certain colors as active and exciting and others as passive and soothing. The active colors are found in the red-blue area. The activity increases with color strength and is additionally strengthened if the red-blue colors are put together with black or blue-black.

Active colors

The passive colors are found in the yellow-green area. Both light and dark values of yellow-green are passive, while intense yellow-green is active and sometimes even jarring when combined with contrasting colors.

Passive yellow-green colors

Passive colors

Active yellow-green colors

The quality of the color

Different colored surfaces can seem related when they have certain common qualities. Surfaces with the same value are clearly related even if they are otherwise different. Surfaces with likeness in value, intensity, tint, shade, and saturation all seem to be related.

Try to describe the similarities and differences of these color

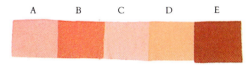

samples; for example: All the samples are reddish, but A and C are bluish-red. C is lighter and clearer than A, which is somewhat grayed. D seems to be equally light as C, but more yellow and less clear than C. B is fairly intense, saturated, and darker than A, C and D. E is oversaturated and the darkest in the row.

The similarity of different surfaces in value is easily read from the color circle as long as they are clear, clean colors. If the colors are pale, unclear or very dark it is far more difficult to determine the value.

The value of the uncolored white, gray, and blackish colors is very easy to determine by comparing with a gray scale. However, it is much harder to determine a strong color's value (see page 120).

By using a scale chart with cut out spaces, it becomes easier to read the precise value of the red samples. You will find then that C, for example, ends up closest to the third step on the gray scale, B is closest to the fifth, and E is closest to the seventh step.

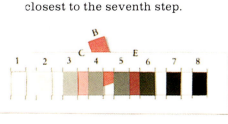

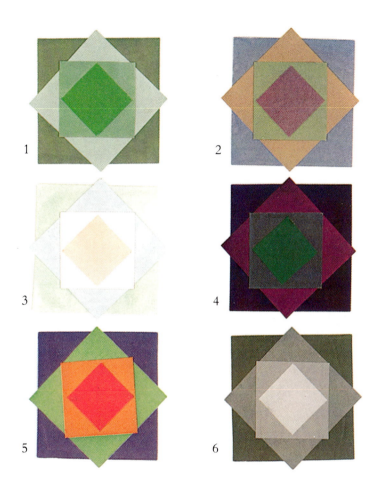

Study the different samples above and try to understand what character the colors in one group have in common before you take part in the analysis to the right.

1
All the squares have the same hue — green with a tint of blue — but different value and saturation.

2
All the squares have different hues, but the same amounts of white, black, and color.

3
All the squares have different hues but the same amount of white.

4
All the squares have different hues but the same amount of black.

5
All the squares have different hues but are the same saturation.

6
All the squares have different values but all are neutral grays.

Color Studies for practical use 129

How colors influence each other

Often colors influence each other so that value, intensity, tone, hue, and so on, change. This phenomenon is called *induction or contrast strengthening*. Knowledge about when or why these changes occur makes it possible to either counteract or take advantage of them.

Simultaneous contrast. When solid colored or uncolored surfaces of different values are adjacent, the differences between them will be increased. In the illustration you will see that the gray area looks darker at the edge of lighter areas and lighter at the edge of darker areas. This phenomenon is called simultaneous contrast. How you read a surface also depends on its form. In the illustration, it looks as if the gray surfaces are curving because of the change in lightness at the borders. If you curve the outer edge, the impression of waviness is further strengthened. You have the impression that there is depth and shadow in the picture.

Reducing simultaneous contrast. The simultaneous contrast or color shifts can be canceled in many different ways, for example, by gradually increasing the intensity of the gray surfaces at the edges or by inserting white or black dividing lines between the surfaces. Inserting narrow stripes with the same intensity as bordering areas will soften the movement from one area to another and will also cancel the contrast. Particularly in weaving, where you sometimes want to create relationships between different areas, moving from one color to another with narrow stripes is very useful.

Black and white surfaces can also be influenced. White can be whiter and black, used together with a color, can take on a hue. The small white rectangle on top of the black field looks whiter than the surrounding white paper. The black squares between the blue ones take on a rust-brown tone.

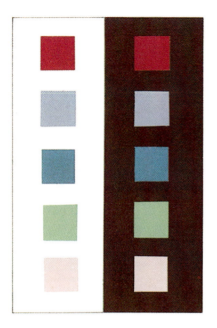

Contrasting values. A light color will look lighter against a dark background or darker against a light background. This is called light induction or value contrast.

Against a black background the colors will show up lighter and more luminous than against a white background. You will also find that the color samples on the black background seem larger than those against the white background, and the white figure against the black back-

ground seems to be larger than the black one, even if they are the same size.

Hue or color contrast. In the illustration of the bowls, both inner areas have the same hue (see the pink strip at the bottom of the picture). However, you can clearly see that the inner area against a blue background seems yellower than the original color, and that it has taken on a warmer, almost luminous tone. Against the surrounding yellowish hue, the inner area seems bluer and cooler. The inner area seems to acquire the surrounding area's contrasting color (see more about contrasting colors on page 134). The size of the inner area compared to the surrounding area and the color strength of the respective areas has, of course, a great degree of influence. If the inner area is large, the surrounding area might change color instead.

Note how the illustration changes. At times you see a bowl on a high pedestal; then at other times you see the profiles of two people facing each other.

Value manipulation. If you want two color areas to have the same value against different backgrounds, you have to tone down the color area which is placed against the dark background. This is a way of counteracting contrast. In the smaller square, you will see how different the two gray color areas must be in order to appear the same against their respective white and black backgrounds.

Color contrasts in gray.
Medium light or light gray shades are especially sensitive to influence by other colors. The pictures of the squares clearly show how a neutral gray area is influenced by surrounding colors. Look, in turn, at the gray squares, which all have the same hue and intensity as the square in the center of the figure. You will find that the gray area placed against a yellow-red background seems bluish, while the one against a green background seems gray-pink, almost violet. The gray square against a red-blue background seems greenish, and the one against a blue background seems yellowish. All together, the gray areas seem to have absorbed some of the surrounding area's contrasting color. The four gray areas placed against a colored background seem lighter than the square at the center.

Knowing the propensity of gray to change like a chameleon, depending on its environment, can be useful in everyday life. For example, if a clear gray sofa is placed against a green wall, the sofa will look gray-pink. The gray color has to be broken with the color of the green background to look clear gray. This is another way of counteracting simultaneous contrast.

Intense color contrast. When a color of medium hue is placed against areas of different color strength, you can clearly see that it will change. Against a background with an intense hue, it will gradually lose its own color strength.

The strength of the hue will also change depending on the size of the area. Most of us have had the experience of selecting color from a small sample in a store and then discovering that it does not live up to our expectations. When painted on large wall surfaces at home the color appears much darker.

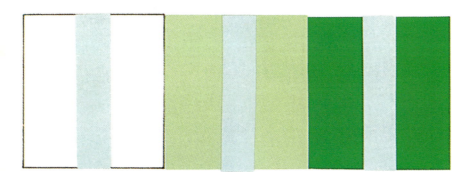

**One and the same color can
seem different.** A color can
change all its qualities depending
on the color next to it.

In the illustration, all the
circles are the same color. See
how they seem to change against
different backgrounds even if
they do, by halves, stand out
against white. The circle seems
stronger in color against a light
green background than against a
dark green one. It acquires an
additional yellow hue against a
blue background, loses its color
strength against a strong green
background, and almost glows
against black.

Even the triangles, which all
have the same color, take on
different characteristics against
the different background colors.
The triangles seem darkest
against the light-green
background, deep green against
blue; they have a muddy
appearance against the clear
green, and become light and
intense against black.

In order to analyze the color
impressions, cover the projecting
parts with white paper. Then you
can easily see the difference
among the green areas.

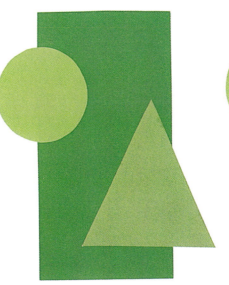

*It is always hard to judge a color if
you don't see it in its proper
context. The wallpaper and the
curtain below, seen separately,
appear to have the same neutral
background color, but when placed
next to each other, the difference in
colors is strengthened dramatically. The background color of the
wallpaper becomes greenish, and
the curtain takes on a rose tone.*

Color Studies for practical use   133

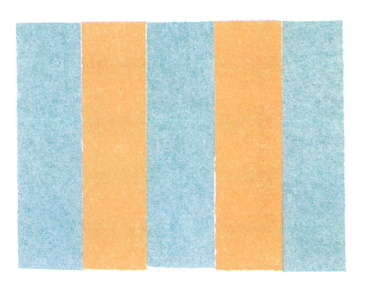

Complementary colors or contrasting colors. Two colors which are opposite each other in respect to hue and which, when mixed produce gray, are called complementary or contrasting colors. In painting, it has long been common to obtain beautiful shades of gray by painting over the first color with a thin layer of its complementary color, or by putting contrasting colors next to each other in lines or dots so the mixing to gray happens first in the observer's eye.

Complementary colors next to each other strengthen the contrast. If complementary colors are mixed

together, they will extinguish each other to produce grau.

This shows the approximate placement or position on the color circle. The complementary color to the yellow primary color is a blue-purple color. Blue has a yellow-orange complementary color, clear red has a green-blue, and clear green has a red-blue complementary color. The contrasting colors yellow/blue-purple are also (like black and white) the contrasts in intensity to each other. With the complementary colors red/blue-green,you will experience a strong contrast between the warm red and the cool blue-green color.

In his color study of 1810, Goethe describes how, with a simple experiment, you can show how the shadow of an object takes on the complementary color to the color of the light that hits the object. By holding different colored filters in front of a candle flame (d), you can vary the color for shadow (b), even if the illumination of the shadow from candle (e) remains the same for the duration of the experiment. A red filter gives a green shadow, blue gives orange, yellow gives purple. Try this simple but effective experiment yourself.

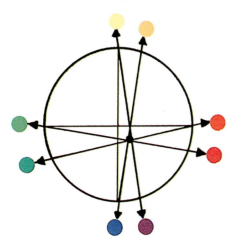

After-images. Look intensely at the red mushroom for 20 seconds. A turquoise corona will start to appear around the mushroom. Then look at a white surface. After a few seconds a turquoise mushroom will appear clearly against the white background. The red mushroom has, so to speak, a turquoise after-image. The after-image will move if you don't have a point on the white paper to focus on.

Now look at the blue cross on the yellow flag for 20 seconds and then move your eyes to the white surface. Then the Swedish flag will appear. The reason for this is that you will see an after-image in colors that contrast with the original picture. The eye tires of being fixed on one color; it wants to find balance and, therefore, developes the contrasting color.

Which flag do you think produces this green and black after-image? Look intently at the black cross for a while. Then move your eyes. You will see the Danish flag. Do your own examples with the flags of other nations.

The eye seems to automatically develop the complementary color to the color we see. The color that appears in this way does not really exist. It can't be photographed. Nevertheless, there are artists who build their paintings on the principal that after-images in contrasting colors will appear on a picture's surface after a period of intense scrutiny.

Canceling the after-image. The after-image can often be troublesome. Take the case of doctors wearing white coats around an operating table. The bright lights and the red blood make them see green dots on their colleagues coats when they look up. When the coats were made of dark green fabric, the after-images no longer appeared and the irritating sight disappeared.

Thus, we can see colors that do not exist! The contrast phenomenon, color changes, after-images, and shadow colors show us that seeing colors is an activity, an unavoidable and unconscious adaption of color impressions.

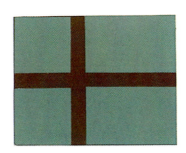

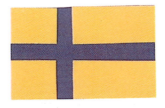

Vibration. Contrasting colors, or cool and warm colors next to each other, can create vibrations and quiverings. Artists often exploit this phenomenon to create life and light in the picture. Vibration is something you want to avoid in your pattern designing. On fabrics meant for clothing it may be irritating, while on printed materials and signs that must be easily read, the vibration would be very distracting.

If you are aiming for a strong color effect but want to avoid vibration, it might be enough to subdue one color. In the two examples on the left with the yellow-red (violet) rectangles, the background has been sub dued in the example on the right, while the figures and the stripes have been allowed to keep their luminosity.

Striped and checked surfaces with strong intensity contrasts also have a tendency to vibrate, especially if the proportions between the light and dark sections are the same, if the stripes are the same width or the squares the same size.

The degree of vibration depends on the density of the pattern and the distance from which it is viewed. The checked surface which vibrates when seen up close will float together and appear gray from a greater distance.

To counteract vibration on striped and checked surfaces, you can change the proportions between light and dark surfaces or lessen the degree of intensity in the pattern. The wider the stripes and the larger the sur- faces, the less vibrating will take place.

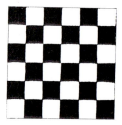

1 2 3 4 5

The importance of color in designing

We have seen earlier that it is the difference in intensity between the different surfaces which most makes a pattern show up clearly.

1

The stripes cut out of paper have a very clear pattern, even if it consists of shades of gray. The four shades are easily distinguished from each other. Now study how the same striping changes character in the yarn wrapping. Your eye reads together the colors which have some common quality, for example, the same intensity (light or dark), the same hue, or the same shades or saturation. Depending on the coloring of the stripes, the pattern may lose its original character, with different surfaces being emphasized from those originally intended. Even here, the distance from which you are looking is of importance. Close up, you might easily read together colors with the same value; from far away, surfaces with the same intensity may read together.

You can not change value in just any way. If you want to change a design from blue shades to yellow shades while retaining the same value, you will soon learn that the yellow tones which correspond to the blues in intensity become very unclear, and the design is not the same.

2

If a small part of the design is given a strong, divergent color, then it is this part, the accent, which will attract the attention.

3

If all the parts of the design are given equal color strength, but in completely different colors, then it is the similarity that will stand out. This will make the design seem unclear and make the rhythm disappear.

4

The same thing applies if the design is colored with different colors, but all in the same weak color tones.

5

If pattern stripes change step-by-step, from darker to lighter hues, the design will become softer and take on a completely different character. The design then has a blurred edge.

Transparency

It is fun to achieve an illusion of transparency using opaque paper. Cut out dark and light, clear and unclear, colored pieces of magazine pages. Partially overlap two pieces and then try to find the possible mixed color of the two pieces. The mixed color has to cover the common surfaces of the two figures. When you have found the correct common mixed color the papers will look transparent. (See more about mixed color on page 150.) All the papers being used in the exercises on these facing pages are completely opaque (not transparent).

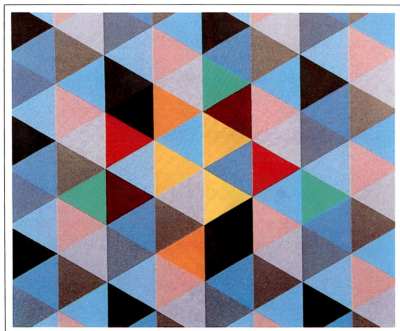

The color combinations in K.G. Nilson's 1976 acrylic painting "Color Building" make some sections seem transparent. Between the different areas, there is constant change and exciting interplay.

In the beginning of the 20th century the Russian avant garde experimented with color and plane, transparency, and mirror image. Sadly, no one took their art seriously, and by mid-century many of them were already forgotten. Thanks to George Costakis' untiring work of tracking down and purchasing works, some have been saved for posterity. At the 1983 show "Russian Vanguards" in Stockholm, you could see, for example, work by two artists who were interested in transparency, Ivan Kljun and El Lissitzky.

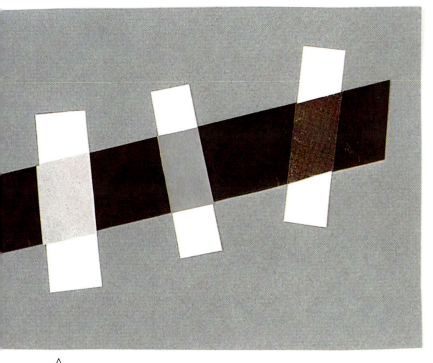

△

It might be hard to decide if the white strip is lying on top of or underneath the black paper. The strip to the right is "clearly" underneath the black strip, while the one to the left is lying on top.

Color composition

A combination of two or more colors is called composition. A color composition is usually experienced as more interesting and more pleasing than the individual color, just as a composition on a piano is a more pleasing experience than the individual note. That we prefer certain colors might depend on learned conventions and earlier experiences where a certain color has played an important role. It is important to exercise your color feelings, and to work without a dislike for certain color fields. One color might be wrong in one relationship but just right in another. Interesting and lively compositions can be created from only one hue by exploiting the intensity, strong and weak tones, tints and shades of the hue (see page 19).

Contrasting colors, which in their maximum strength heighten each others' luminosity and create vibrations, can form quiet, soft, and pleasant compositions if they are chosen in light hues (see page 38 and 66).

1
Using colors from one quadrant, a harmonious composition is formed by all the hues between two adjacent primary colors.
2
Using colors from two octants, the area around a dominant primary color, an animated and harmonious composition is created by using only colors related to the primary color, in this case blue.
3
When combining colors from three or four quadrants, the impression might be too lively and broken due to the increased number of primary colors.

1

It is not feasible to make a list of all possible color combinations. You could say that the more colors that are in a composition the more difficult it is to achieve color balance. To avoid chaotic color effect and divided picture patterns, you should let one color dominate. It is often advantageous if one color dominates in a pattern.

Another way is to give the various colors different character; for example, one color is made lighter, another is made more intense in hue, a third grayed, a fourth more saturated, and so on.

2

3

General information about colors

Light is a basic necessity for seeing colors. In the dark we see no colors. What we ordinarily call light is made up of rays of different wave lengths. The white sunshine is made up of all the colors of the rainbow, from long waves which give rise to red and red-yellow colors to short waves which give rise to blue and violet colors.

Colored surfaces contain pigments which reflect some wave lengths and absorb others. If long-waved light is reflected, we see it as red. If short-waved light is reflected, we see the surface as blue or violet. If all wave lengths are being reflected, we see the surface as white and gray. When the colored light rays pass through the eye, they strike the retina, which, in turn, sends a series of impulses through the optic nerve to the brain.

After a complicated process the nerve impulses reach the visual center of the brain, providing us with color perception.

Colors from mineral substances

Man's inclination to beautify both himself and his environment with the help of color has always been strong, and the art of producing color substances is also very old. The animal pictures in prehistoric caves in France and Spain are painted with earth colors: the values are yellow, red, white, brown and black.

The color substances were crushed in a stone mortar, kneaded with animal marrow, using urine as a binding agent. The colors that had a strong and hardy composition have been preserved right up to the present.

Artists and craftsmen have, for the most part, used color pigments from minerals. For example, yellow ochre, brown umber, terra di sienna (earth from Sienna) came from clay. The same pigments were being used for different kinds of color. If the pigments were bound together with an egg emulsion, the result was tempera colors that were used for wall murals. If the pigments were bound together with oil, the result was oil colors.

Cinnabar, known in China and ancient Egypt, is a yellowish-red color substance that was made principally from the ore of mercury.

Ivory black was made, as the name implies, by burning elephant tusks.

Ultramarine, the only colorfast blue color to which the medieval and renaissance painters had access, was made from the semi-precious stone, lapis lazuli. It was brought from Persia, China and Tibet, that is "beyond the sea" (ultra mare), from which comes the name ultramarine. Many monasteries were known for the manufacture of ultramarine and also for their greed regarding this valuable color.

Sepia, used for wash-drawings, during the Romantic Period, was made from the black-brown fluid secreted by cuttlefish to avoid attacks by its enemies.

Textile colors

For painting textiles, earth colors were first used, either sprayed on with the help of a hollow bone or painted on with a brush. This meant, however, that the colors only lay on the surface and easily wore off. True textile colors first appeared after the discovery of a method to get soluble color substances to penetrate the textile fibers. Discoveries from China, India and Egypt show that this technique was mastered long before Christ was born. The color substances were taken mostly from the plant world. It had been discovered that flowers and leaves, roots, bark, mosses, and lichens possessed useful, and in some cases particularly long-lasting, color substances. Red, yellow, and blue colors were predominant. Green was obtained by first dyeing the material yellow and then dyeing it again with blue. Yellow was less color-fast and bleached easily. The cool blue-green overall tone which often characterized the old tapestries is due to the fact that the yellow colors were less colorfast and bleached. Finally, at the end of the 19th century, it was possible to make colorfast green colors.

Indigo, a blue substance which has been used since earliest times in Asia and, according to Marco Polo, it was known in Venice by the end of the 13th century, can be made from many different legumes. The tropical variety *Indigofera tinctoria,* which comes from India and Java is thought to give the best quality color. Depending on the strength of the dyebath, the indigo gives different colors; everything from greenish-blue over clear blue to bluish-red hues. The hues are always clear and brilliant whether it is a light or an over-saturated bluish tone. Indigo has also been called "the king of colors" because it is especialy beautiful and strong. Now you can get synthetic indigo with the same good qualities.

Indigo

natural material. Current interest in natural dying means that even today you can buy natural indigo.

Woad. From the woad herb, used during the Iron Age for dyeing blues and during the Middle Ages when it was grown on a large scale in Europe (especially in France and Germany), you could get a color substance that looked like indigo but which was considerably less colorfast. Soon the color from woad was strengthened with imported indigo. When the sea route to India was discovered at the end of the 16th century, imported indigo threatened to drive out the use of woad. This resulted in stiff resistance to the use of indigo in the West. During the 18th century when trade became more active, indigo drove out woad completely.

Purple. Around 1600 B.C. a red-hued substance was discovered from the animal kingdom — purple. The color substance was made from juice from the gland of the purple mollusks which were found around the Mediterranean coast. The mollusks were crushed and cooked and then the glandular juice was cleaned and

used for dyeing. When the fabric was dried, a bright dark or bluish-red color appeared which was very colorfast. Purple, which was called "the color of kings," became the most valuable color substance of antiquity and only nobility could afford to wear purple clothing. During Emperor Nero's time, the newborn imperial children were swaddled in purple fabric. No one was allowed to wear a piece of clothing dyed in purple without the emperor's permission. When the Turks conquered Constantinople in the year 1543, the dyers' shops were destroyed and the art of dyeing with purple diminished. Purple is now made synthetically.

Purple was replaced by other red-color substances, two of

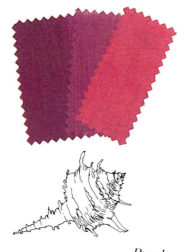

Purple

which also come from the animal kingdom, namely kermes and carmine, both of which were obtained from two different kinds of scale insects.

Kermes from the kermes shield-louse, which for thousands of years had been used to dye red in the Orient, was brought to the Mediterranean world in the

middle of the 15th century.

Carmine, the red color which came from the cochineal scale insect, quickly became important to Europe and is still being used

today. It was already known to the Aztecs and Inca people before the Spanish came to Mexico in 1518. The Spaniards were fascinated by the population's deep red cloaks, whose color greatly surpassed purple. The color substance was extracted from the fertilized female cochineal scale insect which was brushed off its cactus home with a feather. The insects were killed by heating, or with ether, then dried in the sun and crushed in a mortar. By 1526 cochineal were being imported to Europe; in the middle of the 16th century, the Opuntia cactus on which they live was imported as well. Carl von Linne planned to grow the desirable insects in greenhouses in Sweden and in this way to save barrels of gold which importing carmine cost the kingdom every year. When the Opuntia cactus, abundantly covered with insects, was delivered at the Botanic Garden in Uppsala, after an adventurous trip, the package was opened by a garden-master, who only saw small, nasty bugs rather than valuable insects, and flushed them away. When Linne came to inspect his acquisition, there stood the Opuntia cactus, perfectly clean, without a single insect.

Madder, known for thousands of years in Persia and India, became, next to indigo, the most common dye plant in the world. The color substance, which has a healthy yellow-red tone often called "Turkish red" — is extracted from dried root clumps from the *Rubia peregrina.* Karl the Great started many large madder plantings in Europe, and even in Sweden there were madder planta-tions during the 18th century. Cochineal and madder are still in use as dyes today.

Synthetic color. Natural dyes were valuable and exclusive until the end of the last century, when synthetic dyes entered the market. The first synthetic textile colors were made in England in 1856 by an eighteen-year-old student, William Perkin. Towards the end of the 1850s, the larger dye shops on the Continent started producing new dye sub-stances chemically. At first, the synthetic dyes were not colorfast, but today they surpass the natural dyes. The development of synthetic color substances means that we now have an almost unlimited color range at our disposal. With them we can reproduce not only strong, clear and brilliant hues but also the characteristic whole, soft color scale of natural dyes. The fact that the natural dyes are still in use in Sweden to such a large extent is due to a great interest in nature and what it can give us, along with a deeply rooted desire to share in earlier generations' experiences and knowledge, and also perhaps to take part in the comaraderie of the gloriously scented dyebaths.

A brief history of color study

Artists, craftspersons, and dyers have always studied color from both the practical and aesthetic points of view. They prepared their colors themselves, and the recipes for beautiful and colorfast colors were well-kept secrets.

Many authors, philosophers, and observers have been moved to speculate on the differences between color and color ex-perience. The ancient Greeks used to argue whether the color was in the substance or in the mind. Scientists have, in different ways, tried to explain the like-ness and differences in colors, to create systems and laws. Every scientist has been sure of the universal applicability of his theory. Today color knowledge has become a cross-scientific subject which includes chemists, physicists, physiologists, and psychologists.

The renaissance artist, Leonardo da Vinci, was one of the first to write about color. In *The Tract about Painting,* from the end of the 15th century, he talks about six basic colors: white, yellow, green, blue, red and black. His contemporaries did not consider white and black to be colors, but it is these six colors that many of today's scientists think of as the basis for our color system and around which the Swedish color system is built. Leonardo also saw, before anyone else, that shadows have colors.

In 1810, Johann Wolfgang Goethe published a color text on *Zur Farbenlehre,* which is derived from twenty years of study, and is well worth reading even today. Goethe called attention to the importance of experimenting and making your own observations. He discussed "hazy mediums;" for example, smoke looks bluish against a dark background and yellowish-gray against a light background. He also made visual experiments with shadow colors.

The German physiologist Ewald Hering wrote in 1878 that all color systems have to build on how we experience colors — not on how we mix them together. Thus he determined that the basic colors are yellow, red, blue and green.

The American painter Albert Munsell said the important thing was analyzing colors. His system, published at the beginning of the 20th century, was built on five different main colors — red, green, blue, yellow and purple. He organized them according to three observed qualities in a color: tone, strength and shade. This system, which is mainly used in the United States, has been revised many times.

Wilhelm Ostwald, a German professor of chemistry and Nobel prize winner, published a color system in 1917 that is built on four base colors: yellow, red, blue and green. He organized them by their qualities of value, tint and shade. The teaching of Ostwald is sometimes called "color organ."

During the 1940s the Swedish physicist Tryggve Johansson built on the ideas of Munsell, Ostwald, and especially Hering's theories. To create "the natural color system" he started out with four basic colors: yellow, red, blue and green, and organized them according to the color's five observed qualities: hue, value, shade, intensity and saturation. He reproduced them in the graphic symbols of the color circle and the color tone section. White, black, and all the gray tones between, form a lightness scale or gray scale against which the value of the colors is compared.

He also deals with contrast phenomenon, after-images, and color theory in practical use. *The Color Book, Color Teaching for Practical Use,* which the Swedish handicraft organization published in 1965, five years after Tryggve Johannson passed away, is completely built on his theory and the practical study circle work which he pursued from 1948 until his death.

Itten's color circle

About the same time, Johannes Itten, one of the foremost art educators in Europe and a driving force in the Bauhaus ideology, was studying color. He built his color theory, which has attracted a large following, on three basic colors — yellow, red and blue. The picture shows his twelve-section color circle. In the circle, an equilateral triangle and a hexagon are drawn. The triangle shows the three basic colors evenly divided. The hexagon is made up of three triangles which show the mixed colors of the basics — orange, violet and green. His book, *Color and Color Experiences* was first published in 1961.

In 1964, Ingeniorsvetenskapsakademin and the Svenska Slojdforeningen established the Svenskt Fargcentrum foundation, now called the Skandinaviska Farginstitutet. There, under the leadership of economist Anders Hard, a systematic color atlas was created with 1412 precise descriptions of colors which have been adopted as Swedish standards and which have also been accepted in some other countries.

The Natural Color System, NCS, is built on six elementary colors with independent color characteristics — yellow, red, blue, green, white and black. By using simple letter and number combinations to indicate the hue and three variations of the hues, degrees of the color value, tint and shade, one can get unequivocal descriptions of all possible hues. See more about this on pages 126 and 127.

How we use color today

The word "color" has many meanings. Partly, it represents the emotional observation of a color, partly the substance we dip the brush into and then apply to a surface. We use the word "color" (from the French "couleur") when we mean seen and experienced impressions and also to describe the actual charcteristic of the color as being strong, clear, warm, light, saturated, and so on.

When color means the materials to paint with, we often make it clearer by saying the type of paint: water-color, oil-color, lacquer-color, or by saying what the color is going to be used for, such as boat-color, exterior-color, floor-color, and so on.

Through *information* about such things as distance, weather, time

of the year, the health of another person, degree of ripeness of food and freshness which color can provide, color has given human beings the guidance they needed to survive.

Since we read color faster than letters and numbers, it is used for *warning signs* in modern society in almost every field. Think about all the traffic signs with different colors for different kinds of information. In this way, for example, a combination of red, yellow and black is used as a warning.

Color is used in industries and workshops as warning signs. Yellow, often in contrasting diagonal stripes with black, warns of movable machine parts. Red is used for firefighting equipment. Blue means "caution" and is often seen on switches used to start or turn off machines. Green marks protective and safety equipment. A white cross on a green background marks first aid at an accident. A red cross on white background is reserved for the International Red Cross. Exit and emergency signs are often on a red background.

Color markings in the form of lines painted on floors and walls give *directions* and make it easier for patients and visitors to find their way in hospitals and large institutions.

Building standards have many regulations to provide access for handicapped people. One of these regulations is that protruding items in hallways and similar spaces must have divergent colors, *a shocking color as a warning.* These can also be executed in a decorative way.

Color can fool us

For magical and aesthetic reasons, man has since time's beginning used paint to decorate himself and his objects, from cave paintings to today's subway stations, from stone age claypots to today's plastic buckets. New synthetic materials are so gray and boring that for aesthetic reasons they demand color, so, they are being made in red, yellow, green and blue. Natural materials still have a higher status than plastic, which also makes us explore the possibilities at our disposal to use color to change the texture on the object, for example, to make plastic look like wood, metal, or rubber.

With the help of color you can make objects seem heavier or lighter than they really are. Objects seem larger and longer in warm lighting, while they seem shorter and smaller in cool light: blue or green.

You can also use color to change proportions in a room, create an illusion of more space by painting the walls and ceiling in light colors or lower the ceiling height by having the ceiling color extend onto the wall.

Colors help us

Almost one hundred years ago, Florence Nightingale observed that certain colors in the environment helped patients in the field hospital to a sense of well-being and faster healing.

The researchers of today have discovered that the whole body reacts to color. Red lighting increases blood pressure, increases our rate of respiration and the number of eye blinks per second, while blue has the opposite effect. Reaction speed is supposedly 20% faster than normal in red lighting, while green lighting causes slower reactions than normal. We also know that red has a tendency to aggravate symptoms such as nearsightedness and balance disturbances in sick people and that fine motor skills are accomplished with greater precision in green rather than red lighting.

Color as protection

Paint protects objects against weather and wind. Paint is used as a preservative and aging is delayed with a protective coating.

Surfaces can be protected against dirt if they are given a smooth and shiny surface to which the dirt will not adhere. paint can protect against dampness, rot and rust. With a protective coat of paint, a material might last for 100 years, without paint maybe for only ten years. There is paint that protects against fire by forming blisters which insulate the surface from the flames and lower the surface temperature of the wood.

Color for energy conservation

By using a color that gives a feeling of warmth, you can lower the temperature in a room several degrees. A color that reflects light from the walls and ceiling will let you make the lighting more energy efficient. There are colored outer layers which absorb neutrons and protect against radioactive rays. Soon, we might have paint with dust repellant qualities to prevent outer and inner walls from getting dirty. The practical uses for paint will soon have no limits. Even if research and color experience might seem abstract, its observations can often result in practical applications.

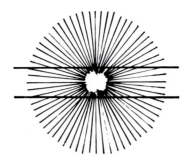

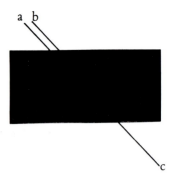

Optical illusions

From experience we know that it is easy to be wrong when we have to give a clear definition of a smell, or something we hear or feel. But what we actually see, we really believe. Look a little closer at the figures on this page and you will soon discover that even your eyes can play tricks on you. The phenomenon depends partially on the fact that the cornea is less curved horizontally than vertically. Therefore, it is impossible to see vertical and horizontal lines sharply on the same plane at the same time.

The Zollner effect. The name comes from the German physicist Friedrich Zollner who, in the middle of the 19th century, observed a street decorated with flagpoles. Around the flagpoles, garlands of leaves had been wound. Zollner did not think the poles were vertically straight. With the help of a plumb-line, he discovered that the poles really were straight. He realized that the garlands were not all wound in the same direction and that this was the reason why at first poles did not seem straight. Two

parallel straight lines seem to bend and get closer to each other at both ends. It is the crosslines, which form larger and smaller angles, which fool the eye.

The three narrow strips seem to be neither straight nor parallel, but if we check with a ruler we will find that it is the slanting lines that lead the eye astray.

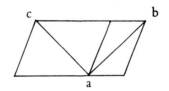

Which one of the two diagonals is longer, a-c or a-b? Most people would say that the distance from a-c is longer than a-b, but actually both distances are of equal length.

The distance between the arrow tips a and b seems less than the distance between b and c. A ruler check will show that both distances are the same.

The Poggendorff figure. Here you have to decide which one of the two lines, a or b, continues in line c. The wide black rectangle distracts the eye, so most of the time we are wrong. Try using a ruler along line c.

Which one of these two pieces is longer? Without hesitation we chose the bottom one, but after measuring you will be more careful concerning the ability of the eye to measure and judge.

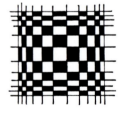

With a gradual change of proportions, a feeling of depth or distance will appear because your eye will focus on the perspective and an optical illusion of volume will appear. Here it seems as it the surface is curving outwards at the center.

Geometric foldings

The quiltmakers of the past and those who did needlepoint have shown how, with a little thought and care, you can fold many geometric forms with paper without the use of a compass, ruler or T-square. Instead, they traced around a saucer or a plate, cut out the form and then folded it into many corners and stars. The Bible was used to draw around, since it was often the only object with a right angle in the home. In this way, they got a rectangle from which they then could fold squares, triangles, rhombuses, and so on. In this way, they produced patterns for sewing.

Place a circle segment reciprocally above and below a line that has been scribed or folded on the fabric, and then draw around the curved line of the segment and you will get an arabesque to decorate.

Fold a circle in half and the resultant half-circle into three equal parts, the circle is now divided into six equal parts. By connecting the intersecting points on the circumference you get a regular hexagon. If the six triangles are turned mirror image outwards, then a six-pointed star is formed.

Fold a circle in half, the resultant half circle in two, and this in two again; the circle will be divided into eight equal parts. The octagon and the eight-pointed star can be formed in this way as the hexagon.

1

Start with a letter-sized paper and fold up one of the shorter sides so it meets one of the longer sides. Then cut off the extending piece of paper: you will have a square.

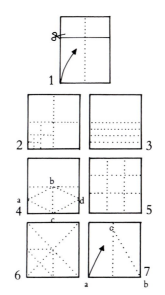

2

Fold a square in half both ways, creating four smaller squares, which in turn can be divided in the same way.

3

Dividing a square in half many times in the same direction forms rectangles and even narrower strips.

4

Dividing a square in half and connecting the center points of the sides on the resultant rectangle by folding, you will have a rhombus, "abdc."

5

Divide a square into three equal parts both ways. You will have the "nine-square" which is very common in quilting patterns.

6

Divide a square diagonally and you will have straight-angled, equilateral triangles.

7

Make an equilateral triangle as follows: Fold the square in half. From corner "b" fold side "ab" up until corner "a" meets the center line at point "c." When "c" is connected with "a" and "b" by folding, an equilateral triangle is formed; "acb."

An oval can be drawn with the help of two push pins, some string and a pencil. The size and form of the oval depends on the length of the string and the distance of the pins from each other.

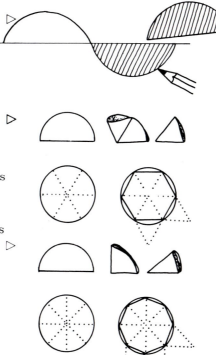

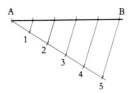

Geometric constructions

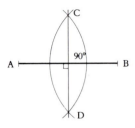

To divide a given length in half with a straight line perpendicular to the given length:

Take the endpoints A and B of the given length as the center-points for two arcs with the same radius greater than ½ AB. They intersect at C and D. Connect C and D. The line CD cuts AB in half and is called the *perpendicular bisector* of AB.

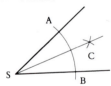

To divide a given angle in half:

S is the vertex of the given angle. Using S as the center, draw an arc that intersects the sides at A and B. Use A and B as the centers for two arcs with the same radius. The arcs intersect at C. The line SC divides the angle in half and is called an *angle bisector*.

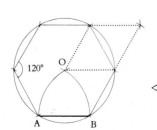

To divide a given length into any number of equal sections:

The given length is AB. Draw a straight line at an arbitrary angle from one end A. Using a compass, mark five segments of equal length on this new line. The length of these sections is arbitrary, but they must be equal. Connect point 5 with point B. Draw lines from 4, 3, 2 and 1 parallel with line 5B. These parallel lines divide the given length into five equal parts.

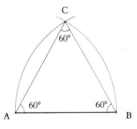

To construct an equilateral triangle with a given length as side:

The given side is AB. Draw two circular arcs with A and B as centers and AB as radius. The arcs intersect at C. Connect C to A and B. ACB is the desired triangle.

To construct a regular hexagon with a given side:

The length AB is the side of the hexagon. Use points A and B as the center points for circular arcs of radius AB. The arcs intersect at O. Use O as the center for a circle of radius OA + AB. Mark the length AB around the circumference of the circle. Connect the points to form a hexagon. By constructing an equilateral triangle on each side of the hexagon you will create a six-pointed star.

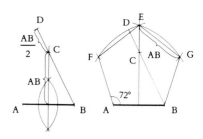

To construct a regular pentagon with one side given:

AB is the given side. Draw the perpendicular bisector of AB and mark the length AB on its giving point C. Connect B and C and extend the line by half the length of AB to D. Take B and A as centers for circular arcs of radius BD. The arcs intersect the perpendicular bisector at E. Mark from E on these arcs the length AB to find G and F. Connect A with F and B with G. AFEGB is the desired pentagon.

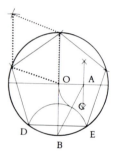

To construct a regular pentagon inscribed in a given circle:

Draw two diameters perpendicular to each other inside the given circle. Divide one radius into two equal parts (A). Connect A with the end point (B) of the other diameter. Use A as the center of a circular arc of radius AO. This arc intersects AB at C. Use B as the center of an arc through C.

This arc intersects the circumference of the given circle at D and E. Connect D and E. Mark this distance an additional four times on the circumference of the circle. Connect the points and you have formed a pentagon. (Five-pointed star, see hexagon.)

Scale

Objects are often reproduced in a size that is either larger or smaller than the real object. The degree of the change is shown in a scale which indicates the relationship between a distance in the picture and the corresponding one in reality. On a map with the scale 1:50,000 each cm or inch corresponds to 50,000 cm or inches, which is 500 meters or 546 yards.

Scale 1:50,000

Scale 1:1 means that the object is reproduced in actual size. Scale 5:1 means the object is enlarged five times.

For practical reasons, you hardly ever make a sketch in actual size. The towels on page 17 intended to be 50 x 70 cm (19¾″ x 27½″), are painted only 5 x 7 cm (2″ x 2¾″). Each cm on the sketch actually means 10 cm. Thus the scale of the sketch is 1:10. If you prefer to work in a somewhat larger size you can sketch in a scale of 1:5. The measurements of the towel, 50 x 70 cm (19¾″ x 27½″) are divided by 5 and the size of the sketch becomes 10 x 14 cm (4″ x 5½″). In a scale of 1:2 the measurement of the sketch becomes 25 x 35 cm (9¾″ x 13¾″).

Scale usually refers to length. Surfaces change on a different relational scale, mathematically called the surface scale, which is the square of the length scale. If the sides of a rectangle are made three times as long, then the surface of the new rectangle becomes nine times as large as the original.

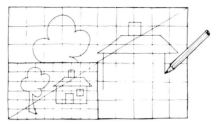

Enlarging and reducing with graph squares

The method of using two graph papers of different scales to enlarge or reduce a picture is very old. You can still find traces of graph-enlarged sketches for the fresco paintings from the end of the 15th century on the walls of Italian cathedrals. Divide the picture you want to enlarge or reduce with vertical and horizontal lines equidistant from each other to form a grid. If one section is especially rich in detail, the squares can be divided into a finer grid to get more supporting lines.

Then place the picture edge to edge at the lower, left side of a larger paper. Draw a diagonal line on the picture and continue across the larger paper. From each point on the diagonal where the line is drawn parallel with the base and height of the picture, a rectangle is formed with the same proportions as those in the picture.

Decide on the size you want for the picture by marking the upper right corner on the diagonal and from this point draw the two remaining sides, producing the desired picture size.

Divide the new rectangle into the same number of squares as the original picture. Then transfer the line pattern of the original picture, square by square, to the larger squares if you are enlarging or to the smaller squares if you are reducing.

Clear plastic with grids can facilitate the enlarging process. This plastic can be bought with black grids in 0.5 (1/4″) or 1 cm (1/3″) squares, but you can draw your own grids on plastic with black projector pen. By placing a grid sheet on top of the picture and another one with larger or smaller scale squares underneath the paper, transferring the work will be a lot faster and you won't have to destroy the picture by drawing lines on it.

In a 1525 woodcut by Albrecht Dürer, the artist is shown viewing his model through a grid stretched in a frame. The artist studies how the lines of the model intersect the grid in the frame and then transfers the lines to his gridded drawing paper. Since the squares on the drawing paper are considerably smaller than those in the frame, he is reducing the scale in the drawing. On the table in front of him, he has a "sighting device" with a small eye at the top through which he is able to watch the model at a constant point. If the artist moves his head, the lines of the model will intersect the framed grid differently.

	yellow	orange	cinnabar	carmine	ochre	burnt siena	yellow-green
yellow							
blue-green							
ultra-marine							
carmine							

Random colors

Test your ability to find the right color by pasting an unevenly cut or torn piece of paper from a colored page in a magazine onto white paper. Then paint around this in such a way that you can't tell where the piece of paper ends and the painting starts. The object is partially to create the right color, partially to duplicate the character of the colored surface.

To "hide the picture" in this way is an entertaining exercise which strengthens your ability to analyze and produce colors.

Color-mixing schematic

You can practice your ability to analyze and render colors quickly by painting a color mixing schematic.

Draw a schematic similar to the one pictured here and color it using all the colors from the paint box including black, white and gray in the uppermost horizontal row. In the left vertical row, fill in the colors of the box in any order you like.

Then, working from left to right, mix all the colors of the box with yellow in the first horizontal row; mix with, for example, blue-green in the second row and carmine in the third row, and so on. Wash the brush well between each color and change the water often.

When the mixing schematic is completed, you will have discovered a great deal about the shades of the elementary colors and, for example, how mixing with white, gray and black can produce a color in a different value area. Yellow and black mixed together give a green color, while a lot of white in a clear blue color will carry the blue toward the green.

You will also discover that colors which lie close to each other on the color circle give clear mixed colors while colors that lie far apart will give unclear, muddy colors. The color mixing schematic can then be used as reference material. You simply compare the color you want to reproduce with the mixing schematic and you can see immediately which two colors to start with. The more colors you mix together, the more muddy the mixed color will become.

Study plan

In Sweden, all study groups which are entitled to state subsidy have to use a study plan which has been approved in advance. Within this framework, the superintendent and the participants have to agree on the objectives and time frame of the study. It is important that the group's work be planned so that as much consideration as possible is given to the participants' expectations, prior knowledge, and time available for homework.

The contents of **The Textile Design Book** covers at least four semesters of studies of the subjects "Color and Composition" and "Shaping," but the book can, of course, be used where applicable for color and composition exercises which are a requirement for handicraft guilds.

The section on color is an adequate base for a separate course in color study. At the first meeting, the course participants need to take part in the study plan and discuss what is most important to begin with. They should realize that each chapter starts out with easy and playful exercises and that the difficulty increases within each chapter and also as the book progresses.

The objectives of the exercises in this book are:

Creative pattern designing with stripes, squares, borders, surfaces and stylized decorations.

Creative pattern designing is built on inspiration, ideas and work. Therefore, you have to train your ability

■ to discover and be inspired by forms, patterns, and color play in nature,
■ to see and be aware of the decorations man has created both in his surroundings and in day-to-day objects,
■ to take part in the rich treasury of patterns collected in books and in museums and historic sites,
■ to be inspired by magazine pictures, everday objects, music, and literature.

We hope the exercises in the book will give both ideas and enjoyment to your work.

Choosing unconventional sketching materials and sketching techniques

Experience with unconventional sketching materials and techniques will be gained from the beginning — sketching objects from nature and using natural fragments — weaving with grass, moss and flowers, making collages with rocks, pine cones and seashells, designing borders with live flowers and leaves, projecting fragments from nature or making shadow pictures from natural objects to find stylized forms for different kinds of patterns.

It might also be inspiring to work with readily available, inexpensive household articles such as heavy brown paper, giftwrap and ribbons, magazine pictures and printed materials. Using these you can cut, tear, paste, paint, braid and weave.

Increasing knowledge of color

The first feelings of pleasure and playfulness in color study exercises show the incredible amounts of colors which the human eye can see and apprehend, and clarify the need for and the advantage of classifying the colors into groups depending on their main qualities. It also treats the color phenomena we encounter in our work with patterns and decorations. It shows how the colors influence and change each other in regard to hue, shade, value, and so on.

The color study informs us of the importance of light, texture and materials in producing color impressions. It shows the importance of light on the different surfaces to the clarity of the pattern; how colors that in one way or another are related to each other blend together, while contrasting colors strengthen the power of brightness for each other and create vibrations.

Color study with different hues demonstrates the attention-getting value in a pattern and even how the pattern changes when viewed from different distances.

Analyzing and interpreting sketches

Your ability to analyze sketches for color, form, rhythm, balance, domination and pattern effect will become trained with ordinary sketching.

Another objective is to train your ability to interpret and to continue developing sketches for execution in different handicraft techniques. You have to train yourself to see the various possibilities of the sketch by cutting it in a suitable way and using "cutouts" to find sections that can be repeated, seen in mirror image or enlarged. You also have to learn to develop idea sketches into working sketches for your chosen handicraft.

Studies of pattern makings from past periods and other cultures

It is important to increase your interest in pattern making and knowledge of past periods and other cultures. This can be done through literature studies, visits to museums, art galleries, photo exhibits, and so on. The participants can themselves take an active part by contributing pictures and objects that show patterns from other periods and cultures. Studies of our own period's patterns and decorations on architecture, printed and woven textiles, and also every-day items such as china, glass, plastics, wallpaper and clothing are also important.

Practical skills

How you train your ability to mix and achieve the right color, how you enlarge or reduce a sketch, and how you work in scale and copy patterns in the easiest way — these are all things the participants need to know at the beginning of the course. These practical skills are among the first exercises in the book.

Geometric constructions are in the book as a review of useful but often forgotten high school knowledge.

In a majority of the exercises, the reporting and designing of patterns are obtained using the mirror image technique.

The possibility of using technical equipment for pattern making depends, of course, on how the classroom is equipped. Most will probably have access to a slide projector.

Group work

Group work provides opportunity for collaboration and discussion, and gives training in composition on larger surfaces, which is otherwise difficult for the lone participant to accomplish during the relatively short time the course lasts. Group work can even lead to a common decoration of the premises.

Homework

The time the participants have for creative exercises during the meetings is relatively short, and therefore, some homework is recommended.

Here are some examples:

■ Continue working with more sketching samples.
■ Make the sketches into practical work by weaving, sewing, painting on china, knitting, woodcarving, and so on.
■ Make your own pattern archives with pictures, fabric samples, newspaper articles, patterned papers, your own sketches from indoor and outdoor museums and historic sites.
■ Review the history of past periods' color materials to the present usage of color. Also read the other historic and "fun to know" sections in the book.
■ The bibliography lists books for further study. Even in books that deal with other handicraft media than your own, you can be inspired and learn something about how patterns and decorations adapt to form, materials and objects.

Group work
Stripe becomes square following the "Africa method"

In Africa they weave long narrow strips with alternating patterned and solid colored sections. When the strips are then sewn together into larger fabric pieces, the patterned and solid areas are displaced to form complicated square patterns.

The exercise below is built on the same idea. The participants in the group each get a letter-sized sheet of paper, white or colored, which they have to cut in half lengthwise. Each strip is folded in three equal sections, lengthwise. Each section has to be decorated as follows: one strip has the center section decorated with stripes across, the other strip is decorated at the outer sections. Limit the number of colors and choose a color that must be used by all participants in their stripes. Join all the strips together so that striped sections alternate with solid-colored sections. Then a checked surface will appear with alternate squares being striped. Solid-colored squares can then be decorated with simple geometric forms. (See the sketch of an African weaving on page 29.)

Diagonals form squares

Paint two letter size papers with diagonal stripes, one with stripes from the bottom left slanting to the right and one with the stripes from the top left to the right. Choose a color that must be used in the stripe patterns of all the participants. Have some students paint narrow stripes and some wider stripes.

Experiment to see which

stripes will go together before the papers are cut into small squares, rectangles, or narrow strips. Turn the pieces around so that the stripes meet at the center of the new squares that are formed when the pieces are joined together (see the rug sketch on page 46). Paste the pieces on a solid-colored background with a predetermined space in-between which will tie the design together. The

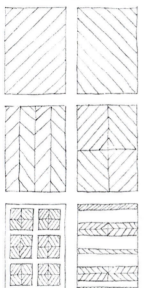

diagonally striped papers can also be used as a background for larger, solid-colored surfaces or figures. Experiment and use your imagination.

Borders make a frame

Here you have to create a colored frame for a solid-colored, rectangular, center surface by putting border next to border. It can be filled with a text of some kind — an award, a proverb, a quotation or something similar.

Any border shown in the chapter "Borders" can be reworked into a frame. Choose both light and dark colors that harmonize with each other and with the solid-colored center section. The borders don't need to be the same on the long and short sides; both pattern and width may vary. Narrow, solid-colored stripes or strips might be needed between the borders to hold them together for a frame.

The picture with the proverb on page 68 shows borders put together with patterned and unpatterned paper. Dots and stripes are added with a gold pen.

Many Oriental rugs are built on the composition principle of placing border next to border. Try to design a rug in this way.

Stamp printing makes a surface

When the potato printing exercises are completed, the group, working together, can use the stamps to illustrate a poem, a mood, or a time of the year. First plan the surface for the coloring and designing before you start printing with the stamps. Completely ignore the shape of the stamps, but choose color care-

fully and print with shading and overprinting (see page 82 and 83). In this way you might create a design which fits the subject you chose.

The picture shows a group work where the participants in a "picturesque" way tried to illustrate Ingrid Sjostrand's poem:

"On paths
one never walks
completely alone.
The feet have company from
all the steps that
have stepped
along the path."

Composition exercises using stylized flowers

Let flowers from the field or garden be the theme. All the participants form flowers with long pipe cleaners or thin wires. This produces soft stylized forms and since all the pipe cleaners or wires are equal in length, all the flowers will be about equal size. (Compare the exercise with animals on pages 114 and 115).

Place the completed flowers on top of a large white paper and choose several to continue working with. Trace them onto

transparent paper. Decide on four or five colors to be painted on paper which will be cut so that everyone can get color samples. Each person then paints at least three samples of her flowers in these colors so together you have a bunch of flowers to "play with." Cut out the flowers but leave a little extra around the edges so they last while being handled. Now try either to spread out the flowers in dense or sparse surface patterns, or to gather them for a wreath or a bouquet to put in a pot. Trace the different solutions onto transparent paper so the compositions are preserved, or document them by photographing them. Then choose different techniques for execution. The surface patterns might be printed, the pot embroidered, or the wreath appliqued. The painted flowers can again be pinned to the walls in the room so that new course participants can arrange them in a different way.

Enlarging and color matching

With this amusing and useful exercise, the group can practice enlarging and matching colors.

Cut a picture into a number of sections and in such a way that something is "happening" in each section. Each participant receives her own section and must (without looking at the others' sections and without looking at the original picture) enlarge her section to double the size using the graph method (see page 149). It is important to be as careful as possible both with the enlarging and color matching (see page 150), since all the sections have to be reassembled for a large picture.

The group work of the color

study "How pink is the pig" and "The color wheel of flowers" are found on page 121 and page 125, respectively.

Practical hints for carrying out the exercises

With weft from nature (page 6). For the warp you can use thin wrapping string, cotton warp yarn, or unbleached linen yarn nr. 16/2. Warp length should be about 8 meters (8¾ yds).

You can hang the weavings on the classroom wall and compare them to each other. The personal choice of materials, colors, and working method will ensure that none of the weavings look the same.

Shadows and silhouettes (page 9). The projector can be focused on larger objects so they make shadows on the wall. Dried seed-pods, grass, ferns and elegant twigs will give very beautiful shadows which may be traced.

Impressions (page 10). To make a plaster cast of the impression on a clay tile you need to built up an edge of clay or sturdy cardboard around the tile. Pour on thin, runny plaster to about a 2 cm (¾") thickness. Let the plaster harden. Then carefully remove the paper or clay edge and then loosen the plaster relief from the tile.

Collage with objects from nature (page 10). As a base for the collage you can use masonite or sturdy cardboard. Limit the size to 15 x 15 (6" x 6") and glue with wood glue. Hang the collage on the wall as a decoration and as an inspiration for future exercises.

Stripes inspired by objects in nature and from pictures (page 15). Use double cardboard pieces when you are winding stripes with yarn. If you tuck the ends of the yarn between the

cardboard pieces when you begin and end a color, it is fastened automatically.

Painted stripes (page 17). When painting towels, it is practical to draw many rectangles at one time. A common towel measurement is 70 x 50 cm (27½" x 19¾"). If you work in a scale of 1:10, the rectangles are going to be 7 x 5 cm (2¾" x 2"). Paint with a flat brush which will give you both wide and narrow stripes.

Creating completely different stripes with the same amount of color (page 19). Paint with the colors in the same proportions as in the source of inspiration (1). A suitable paper is letter size. Cut the paper into three equal sized pieces directly across the color fields (2), which gives you a base from which to cut strips from three completely different stripe patterns.

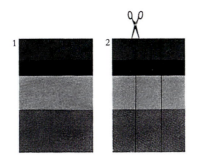

Cut outs (page 22). Make the model by cutting out the form of a pot, sweater, chair, tote bag, hat or mittens in a heavy white paper. Slide the cut out across the sketch. In the cut out form you will see what portion of the design looks the best.

Stripes from memories (page 23). It might be hard to cut very narrow stripes for a rug sketch. Instead let the strips be on top of

each other so that one you want to be narrow is on the bottom and only peeps out. If you have access to an enlarger, you can project the "rug" on the wall in full scale (1:1) to see if the proportions are pleasing.

Stripe as a picture (page 28). Often the size of the paper will limit the size of the sketch, but it is good to not be bound by the size of the sketch; on the other hand, imagine the sketch to be both monumental and miniature in size.

Word inspired square pattern (page 34). The character of a soft material can be achieved in many different ways.

You may:

- Paint wet on wet so the colors run together.

- Use paint or crayons on coarse, uneven paper.

- Color with oil-based crayons and then smear the color with your fingers.

- Draw with water-based magic markers or watercolors on slightly damp paper.

Determine which technique suits your medium the best.

Letter borders (page 69). Make many copies of a letter border and color them in different ways. Study the colorings for the denseness of the pattern, the balance, readability, usefulness, and so on. Make the borders mirror image, or stack them on top of each other and form surface patterns in this way.

Tissue paper cutting (page 73). Tissue paper is inexpensive and easy to work with, but the color will fade quickly. Tissue paper is most easily pasted with wallpaper paste, applying the paste with a wide, flat brush. First brush the paste onto the base paper, lay the tissue paper on top and smooth it out with the help of the wide, flat brush. Brush on paste between each layer of tissue paper.

Potato printing (page 80). Potatoes are a perfect material for making printing stamps. They are inexpensive, have just the right firmness and are easy to work with. One disadvantage is that the stamps are not durable. They can be saved for a few days in a tightly sealed plastic bag, but then they will shrivel. This has the advantage of forcing you to make new stamps and new patterns.

A good potato stamp must have a completely flat cut surface. Therefore, cut the potato in half with a large, sharp knife. The pattern is cut out with a small, pointed knife; the scores can be made with a hair clip. To make sure that the design is right side up when printing, you can cut a mark showing the direction on the top of the potato. Narrow stems can be printed with a thin potato slice which can be bent with light pressure. For mirror image you will need two stamps. Brush paint on the first stamp and press it onto another sliced potato half and cut out the pattern. Numbers and letters must always be cut in mirror image on the stamp to be correct when actually printing.

Stamp combinations (page 80). It might be fun to combine different stamps in the same pattern. It is easier if the stamps are similar in size in at least one direction. Here are stamps of a square, a triangle, and a circle that have been put together. The narrow scores are cut with a hair clip.

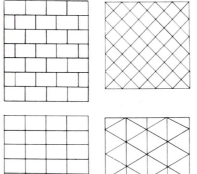

Surface patterns with the help of a grid (page 88). Here you can see some suggestions for grids. You can draw them yourself in the scale you like.

Stylizing (page 100). To transfer a drawing onto black or colored paper, you can first draw on the back of the drawing with an oil-based crayon in a color that will show up clearly on the paper to which you are going to transfer the drawing. The crayon layer

works as carbon paper. You may also use tracing paper sold in fabric stores. It is available in many colors.

Designing with pipe cleaners (page 115). Shown above are a few examples of how the circularly formed animals can be put together depending on the intended use of the composition. You may also color them freely with bright colors.

The colortone field (page 126).

With the help of the figures and the text below, you will learn to analyze and describe the hue and value, tint and shade.

The most prominent quality of a color is called its primary tendency and the less prominent quality is its secondary tendency.

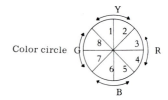

Color circle

Area 1 - 2 yellow is dominant
  1 secondary tendency greenish
  2 secondary tendency reddish

Area 3 - 4 red is dominant
  3 secondary tendency yellowish
  4 secondary tendency bluish

Area 5 - 6 blue is dominant
  5 secondary tendency reddish
  6 secondary tendency greenish

Area 7 - 8 green is dominant
  7 secondary tendency bluish
  8 secondary tendency yellowish

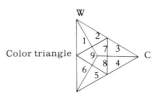

Color triangle

Area 1 - 2 white is dominant
     3 - 4 coloring is dominant
     5 - 6 black is dominant

7 White + coloring is dominant, black secondary tendency
8 Coloring + black is dominant, white secondary tendency
9 White + black is dominant, coloring secondary tendency

Materials

Paper
- Different kinds papers (colored, white, gray and black) on which to paint and draw, to cut models from and to make sketches.
- Plant-pressing paper or some other lightly absorbent paper for paint or imprinting with potatoes.
- Cardboard to wind yarn around or to "weave" on.
- Graph paper; 0.5 cm (4 to the inch) and 0.25 cm (16 to the inch) squares for sketches and working drawings.
- Transparent worksheets for copying and mirror image exercises.
- Tissue paper in many colors.
- Brown wrapping paper, wallpaper, giftwrap, corrugated cardboard and other kinds of wrapping paper.
- Colored pictures from magazines, travel brochures, and so on.

Color
- Oil-based crayons.
- Water colors.
- Paint.

Pens
- Pencils in different degrees of hardness.
- Water-based felt tip pens (for color drawings).
- Colored pencils.
- Projector pens (permanent ink) in different sizes.

Brushes
- Round paintbrushes in different sizes.
- Flat paintbrushes in different widths.
- Painting sponge or dauber (see page 92).
- Roller.

Plastic
- Plastic folders to store your sketches in, cut stencils from, and draw patterns on.
- Clear, graphic plastic for enlarging.

Other materials
- Scissors, ruler, compass, T-square, eraser, gluestick, wallpaper paste, tape, hobby knife, two rectangular mirrors without frames, long pipe cleaners or soft wires, different kinds of yarn, sewing thread, tapestry needles.
- Slide projector and glass slide frames.
- Enlarger and, if possible, copier.

Index